FOLLOW THE MONEY

FOLLOW THE MONEY

The Money Trail Through History

RUBEN ALVARADO

WordBridge
PUBLISHING
εν αρχη ην ο λογος
AALTEN, THE NETHERLANDS

THE COIN PRESENTED on the cover (both front and back, showing the obverse and reverse) and on the title page is an English two-guinea gold coin, minted in 1677 during the reign of Charles II. The coin is representative of a fundamental shift in monetary policy that changed the course of Western civilization.

Cover photography courtesy Lawrence Chard: chards.co.uk.

THE REPRESENTATIONS of the coins on the cover and in the text correspond as closely as ascertainable to the actual sizes thereof.

THE ILLUSTRATIONS PRESENTED in the text are all in the public domain.

www.wordbridge.net

TABLE OF CONTENTS

ACKNOWLEDGMENTS

This book benefitted greatly from the editorial expertise of Natalie Peters.

To
Dr. Gary North
who (among other things)
taught me the importance of "the bankers"

1. INTRODUCTION

"Defense of the dead is not the main purpose of historical writing; its greater purpose is to make the past known and understood in the most meaningful terms provided by subsequent experience. New concepts and new information call for new narratives."[1]

This is a book about money. Not about how to make it, or to bemoan the fact that it must be made. It is a book about money as the motive force underlying human society, acting in subterranean fashion because misunderstood, misrepresented, or just missed. Money is taken for granted without realizing the powerful influence it has.

There are economists enough who would have us believe that money itself is unimportant; it is but a surface phenomenon obscuring the underlying reality of a supposed "real economy." They are sadly mistaken.

Money goes a long way to determine not only a society's economic performance, but even its world-view: the way people think, the way they act, the hopes they have, the fears they harbor. Although this book is not a history of mental states, the topic will often make its presence felt. And the interesting thing is, as enlightened as we fancy ourselves to be, we are still unaware of the effect that money has on us.

The current political climate provides a classic example. We hear from both the left and the right side of the political aisle that the ultimate cause of the current economic malaise is greed, centered in the financial and banking sector. We have been led to believe that Wall Street traders and big bankers pursued profits at the expense of the common good, creating a massive asset bubble that burst with spectacular effect in 2008. And since then, these same culprits have been receiving monies from government in order to survive the economic disaster they themselves brought upon us, while ordinary citizens are laid off or go bankrupt without the prospect of any such bailout to keep them in their job or business.

---

[1]Bray Hammond, *Banks and Politics in America from the Revolution to the Civil War* (Princeton: Princeton University Press, 1957), p. 287.

Such a critique is nothing new. In fact, it is borrowed from a bygone age (the age of the Money Power or "finance capitalism"), an age which came crashing down during the "Great Transformation" – the focus of chapter 14 – the major events of which were the Great Depression and World War II. In those days, it was indeed the financial and banking powers that held a tight grip on power and policy and directed the world into disaster. But their power was broken then, and they no longer wield the power they once had. The political rhetoric condemning "finance capital," however, has lived on, and is dusted off and brought to bear whenever financial problems of any serious magnitude are faced. That rhetoric remains a strong component of the extreme right-wing and left-wing political vocabulary at all times. But the conditions that justified the use of that vocabulary have changed drastically.

The basis for that power, and that rhetoric, was metallic currency. During the age of the Money Power, this currency was gold. For the preceding "Age of Mercantilism," it was both gold and silver. The fact that money was composed of precious metals – "specie" – rendered it a scarce resource, and inspired a primal urge to hoard and a fanatical intent to acquire and preserve privileges, and to resist change rather than embrace it. This urge fed the demand for acquired, state-provided entitlements. The age of mercantilism was in fact the age of privilege, up and down the social scale. The state – the king – existed to establish and confirm outcomes, even to ensure them. Behind this panoply of privilege, it was the overriding need to ensure security, in the face of the fluctuating supply of precious metals, that inspired the mania for protectionism that characterized mercantilism.

The philosophy behind this state of affairs is the zero-sum game: a fixed amount of wealth, which must be allocated by the central authority, and to which the various interest groups in society lay claim, the more forceful and powerful obtaining a greater share, the less powerful a lesser one. This orientation becomes elevated to the status of world-view, timeless eternal verity, as best exemplified in Montaigne's essay, "That the Profit of One Man is the Damage of Another."[2] What is not recognized is that this

---

[2]In Michel de Montaigne, *The Essays of Montaigne,* trans. Charles Cotton, ed.

orientation is no timeless condition but the product of circumstances, viz., monetary scarcity. Such scarcity was *de rigueur* during the age of mercantilism, as shall be explored at length in this book. The question is, is such still the case?

The age of mercantilism was followed by the age of the gold standard and fractional-reserve banking. Money, in the form of bank credit, was made available in ever-multiplying amounts; but the specie basis for the money supply was narrowed down to gold. And it was ultimately the availability of gold, or lack thereof, that determined the supply of money, price levels, and economic growth rates. And gold, being the scarce commodity that it is, ensured that the regime of monetary scarcity would continue. One of the consequences was that the labor force was made to shoulder the burden of deflationary adjustments brought on by recurrent periods of monetary shortage. To this condition we owe the advent of the modern age of labor legislation.

So – scarred by these centuries-enduring experiences of monetary scarcity, we still carry the zero-sum mentality with us, even though the basis for it has vanished. For money itself has changed absolutely. It is no longer the fickle, here-today-gone-tomorrow phantom it was in the day of Spanish pieces of eight, English guineas, or Venetian ducats. Nor is it subject to specie-driven deflationary collapses, the way it was in the days of the gold standard. In other words, our economic condition and positions no longer demand a central role for government-conferred privileges, because with the change in money, there comes a change in the need for those privileges. After all, they had their reason for being within a scarce-money regime. Today, with our money supply capable of expanding in accordance with broader economic conditions, we have need of general, common-law

---

William Carew Hazlitt (London: Reeves and Turner, 1877 [1580]). Ludwig von Mises went so far as to label this way of thinking *the Montaigne dogma:* "It is at the bottom of all modern doctrines teaching that there prevails, within the frame of the market economy, an irreconcilable conflict among the interests of various social classes within a nation and furthermore between the interests of any nation and those of all other nations." *Human Action: A Treatise on Economics* (Auburn, AL: Ludwig von Mises Institute, 1998 [1949]), p. 660.

protections of property and contract, which allow for change and entrepreneurial "creative destruction" rather than inhibit it.

At least, such ought to be the case. But, as everyone can see, we have
embarked on a new, seemingly unprecedented journey, characterized as the
"New Normal." There is once again a perceived need for government and
its privilege-extending protectionism and provision of benefits in the face of
a seemingly unforgiving economic environment.

The truth of the matter is, while we have once again embarked on a
scarce-money trajectory, this time the basis for it is not a scarcity of monetary materials, but various monetary and fiscal policies conducted by countries in order to promote their own perceived national interests, but which,
in an eery echo of the late-1920s-early-1930s, jointly make for a poisonous
global economic environment. This is a subject for another book, one on
which the present author is already at work; but enough can be said now
firmly to locate the present condition within the framework of this book,
oriented as it is toward explaining the past.

Monetary manipulation has led to a condition of scarce money – an
artificial condition, but a real one for all that. The road to our current
scarce-money situation has been boom-bust, asset bubbles, similar to what
preceded the Great Depression (to wit, the Roaring Twenties), to what
happened in Japan in the late 1980s (from which that country still has not
recovered), and to what gave us the credit crisis of 2007-2009, which is
directly responsible for the situation today. The excess liquidity in the first
decade of the 21st century was generated mainly by the combined efforts of
the Bank of China and the Federal Reserve, producing what Lombard
Street Research has dubbed the "New Dollar Area" – "an informal, fixed,
or semi-fixed exchange rate regime centered on the dollar," which, "whatever it is called, … did much to cause the world financial crisis."[3] This New
Dollar Area, along with the European Monetary System, with its shared
currency, the euro, have led to the global imbalances and excess liquidity
that were the fuel behind the asset bubbles in the USA, Spain, Portugal,

[3]Brian Reading, "New Dollar Area: The Makings of the Mess," available at
http://www.qfinance.com/capital-markets-viewpoints/new-dollar-area-the-maki
ngs-of-the-mess?full.

Greece, Ireland, and wherever else. So it wasn't nefarious bankers that were behind the boom and bust – it was monetary policy, with a predilection for fixed exchange rates, a predilection to control the money supply for the sake of ulterior goals. Excess liquidity provided a misleading boom, for it was only the symptom of a deeper maldistribution (hence "imbalances"). That maldistribution had eventually to find a fresh equilibrium; and because it was artificially restrained, the final burst was akin to a dam breaking. Economic fundamentals had been distorted to such an extent as to cause entire economies to bust up and freeze up. The result is the current situation of tightness, a "balance-sheet recession,"[4] even in the face of near-zero short-term interest rates.

Despite the appearance, our monetary system is not one of scarcity but of abundance. Eventually, it will recover, when bad policies are reversed. It took centuries to arrive at such a monetary system. We take it for granted, but we shouldn't – look where that has gotten us. This system is a delicate artifact. It is the expression of a social order which itself is anything but a "natural state," and can never be assumed as pre-existing. Civil society itself is the product of a lengthy evolutionary process, a product of human action, but not of human design.[5] It is a society formed of free and equal individuals combining through myriad organizations, corporations, and other voluntary associations, in which family and church play an essential transgenerational role. The state exists to guarantee these individuals, within the context of this multilayered organizational life, in their rights of property and contract, sustained by the rule of law.[6] This society has as its reflex a monetary order based in abundance. As such, it does not seek to preserve past acquisition at the expense of future opportunity, but to guarantee both.

---

[4]On the subject of balance-sheet recessions, see Richard Koo, *The Holy Grail of Macroeconomics: Lessons from Japan's Great Recession* (Singapore: John Wiley & Sons (Asia) Pte. Ltd., 2009.

[5]This aphorism of Friedrich Hayek's was first put forward by the 18th century Scottish philosopher Adam Ferguson: see Russell Roberts, "The Reality of Markets." September 5, 2005. Library of Economics and Liberty. Accessed at http://www.econlib.org/ library/Columns/y2005/Robertsmarkets.html.

[6]I have written extensively about such a society in Alvarado, *Common Law & Natural Rights: The Question of Conservative Foundations* (Aalten: WordBridge Publishing, 2009).

For the zero-sum game is a contrivance to deal with a situation that is artificially created and can be overcome.

On its own, money cannot guarantee a good result. What *can* guarantee such a result is these institutions of civil society, along with free and conscious citizens aware of the situation and acting accordingly, animating those institutions. These alone yield the result of a prosperous, enterprising, ever regenerating society. And yet money goes a long way to make that result possible, just as it went a long way to make other societal forms possible. That is the gist of the story that lies ahead.

It is a story that, in Hammond's words cited above, could only be made possible by "new concepts and information," calling for "new narratives." The new concepts and information are embodied in the wide-ranging body of scholarship of which I have been privileged to make use. All I have done is string together into a coherent whole the myriad pieces, themselves produced with true scholarly effort and strenuous attention to detail. Obviously, this story could not have been written without them. It is my hope that it will do justice to all of that effort, and, indeed, make more sense of those individual efforts than ever could be achieved in separate existences, each in splendid academic isolation.

PART I
ANCIENT MONEY

2. THE UNIVERSAL GLUE

The story of money begins when history itself begins, where, as a sort of premature epitaph, stands the Tower of Babel. The Tower tells us that mankind's ideal is unity; it also tells us that mankind's practice is fragmentation.

Correspondingly, there are two movements at work in history – particularism and universalism, or, fragmentation and unification. Particularism is the practice, universalism the ideal.

Although unity through the brute force of conquest was always being attempted, only one thing successfully drew the disparate masses into constructive communication with each other. This was *money*, specifically the precious metals gold and silver.

Why did money originally take this specific form? The reason is intimated in J.R.R. Tolkien's allegorical epic *The Lord of the Rings.*[7] At the heart of Tolkien's saga lies the quest for unification in the face of fragmentation.

The means of unification is a ring with the giveaway name, the Ring of Power. This ring, the story goes, is at the heart of a cluster of rings distributed amongst the various denizens of Middle Earth – elves, dwarves, and men. The holder of the Ring of Power holds the possessors of the other rings in his grasp. "One ring to rule them all, one ring to find them, one ring to bring them all and in the darkness bind them ..." runs the spell. Sauron, the forger and holder of the Ring of Power, exercises the ring's power over the lesser rings. In the story, that power obviously is magical. But there is also an allegorical dimension that speaks to historical reality. And this has to do with the *composition* of the rings.

Tolkien's Ring of Power is a ring of pure gold. The rings over which it has power are rings of bejeweled precious metals. And the power that these precious metals exercise over men is a power that is derived from voluntary submission. It is not mere imposition upon and subjugation of the will that is involved here, but the *agreement* of the will. The holders of the

---

[7]Allegorical because it captures themes derived from actual history, while clothing them in the garb of myth and legend.

rings desire them, and submit to their power *voluntarily*. They desire them, at least in part, merely for the material from which they are made.

This is a theme that echoes throughout all the ages of history, across all human boundaries, and within all human cultures. The precious metals have taken their place as money and the means for realizing unification because they possess a universal attraction. The capacity to embody value has allowed these metals to be put to use as currency. They have thereby become the great tool by which communication between the fragmented shards of humanity has been realized.

This communication enabled the various superfluities of each region to be exchanged one for another. Precious metals, capable of embodying and storing high levels of universally-recognized value, catalyzed these exchanges, and so made possible the formation of an economic world-order. Their great value has been their service as universal glue.

Thus was ensconced a regime which proved decisive throughout the course of history. The precious metals became the focus of concentrated value, precisely through the function they performed as an indisputable means of communicating value across boundaries. This position at the fulcrum of the economy, together with the concentrated value they embodied, transformed the precious metals from a mere accouterment, a status symbol, into a veritable tool both embodying power and capable of being wielded in the acquisition of further power.

How did this power complex develop? A look at ancient empires provides answers.

Early on, there were two main foci of empire: Mesopotamia and Egypt. Each was the product of great rivers: the Tigris and Euphrates in Mesopotamia, the Nile in Egypt. These alluvial plains harbored great potential for sustaining life, but that potential could only be exploited on a collective, rational basis. The result was, in the characterization of V. Gordon Childe, an "urban revolution."

> In a small tract no larger than Denmark, on the Tigris-Euphrates delta, the ancient Sumer (Shinar in the Bible), the transformation can be followed step by step in the archaeological record. Sumer was new land only recently raised above the waters of the Persian Gulf by the silt carried down by the two rivers. It was still

covered with vast swamps, full of towering reeds, interrupted by arid banks of mud and sand, and periodically inundated by floods. Through tortuous channels among the reeds the muddy waters flowed sluggishly to the sea. But the waters teemed with fish, the reed brakes were alive with wild fowl, wild pig, and other game, and on every emergent patch of soil grew date palms offering every year a reliable crop of nutritive fruit.

By contrast to the arid desert on either side, this jungle must have seemed a paradise. If once the flood waters could be controlled and canalized, the swamps drained, and the arid banks watered, it could be made a Garden of Eden. The soil was so fertile that a hundred-fold return was not impossible.[8]

This transformation was indeed accomplished, resulting in a luxuriant growth of cities and towns. There then arose an inconclusive struggle for hegemony between them. "Though all the cities of Sumer and Akkad enjoyed a uniform culture and though, or because, all were dependent on the waters of the same rivers, each was politically independent and ready to fight its neighbours."[9] In Egypt, by contrast, came the triumph of Pharaonic hegemony.

Trade was the vehicle by which these disparate communities maintained rapport amongst each other. And, as conducted in the ancient world, it was mainly an aristocratic activity. "The surplus produced by the new economy was, in fact, concentrated in the hands of a relatively small class."[10] In both Babylonia and Egypt, the main form of economic organization was the large-scale estate. In Babylonia this took the form of large temple and palace complexes. These formed large economies in their own right which were capable of providing most of the necessities of life for the many dependents, minimizing the role of local markets, and making market essentially a long-distance, "wholesaling" affair.

---

[8]V. Gordon Childe, *What Happened in History* (New York: Penguin Books, Inc., 1946), pp. 82-83.

[9]Childe, *What Happened in History*, p. 92.

[10]Childe, *What Happened in History*, p. 92.

The market, then, primarily involved dealings between these large-scale producers and consumers, involving both raw materials and luxury items. It was necessary to the existence of these river-based civilizations; as Graeber puts it, "[the caravan] trade was crucial because while the river valley of ancient Mesopotamia was extraordinarily fertile and produced huge surpluses of grain and other foodstuffs, and supported enormous numbers of livestock, which in turn supported a vast wool and leather industry, it was almost completely lacking in anything else. Stone, wood, metal, even the silver used as money, all had to be imported."[11]

The aristocratic orientation was strengthened by structural factors, mainly metallurgy and writing. Up until around the turn of the first millennium before Christ, bronze (a copper alloy) was the main metal used for tools and weapons, giving this period the name of the Bronze Age. By this very fact, tools and weapons were restricted to a small minority, because copper was a relatively scarce commodity, and metallurgy had not yet attained the capacity for working other metals requiring more advanced techniques, involving higher temperatures. Therefore, "an actual or virtual monopoly of metal armament placed the pharaoh, the king, and the city-governor – the personifications of the Egyptian and Sumerian [i.e., Babylonian] States – in an almost impregnable position."[12] As far as writing was concerned, it was conducted mainly in cuneiform or hieroglyphics, both of which used pictographs to represent words. Because of this, only a restricted corps of scribes could master the written language, which kept reading and writing from spreading among the masses.

Trade linked these islands of economic activity together; and trade was conducted on the basis of commodity currency. The commodity that triumphed was silver, and to a lesser extent gold,[13] forming the backbone of

---

[11]David Graeber, *Debt: the First 5,000 Years* (New York: Melville House, 2011), p. 64.

[12]Childe, *What Happened in History*, p. 125.

[13]"Silver eventually won the day. It was not only more durable and more constantly in demand than the other 'exchangeable commodities,' but also had the virtue of being easily carried about the person because of its high value per unit of weight. This was theoretically also true of gold, but gold was generally from seven to ten times as valuable as silver, in other words *so* valuable that it was impractical to carry about. It was used as money only in the Middle Babylonian period." Wil-

an extensive network of international trade. "For much of human history … an ingot of gold of [sic] silver, stamped or not, has served the same role as the contemporary drug dealer's suitcase full of unmarked bills: an object without a history, valuable because one knows it will be accepted in exchange for other goods just about anywhere, no questions asked."[14]

By this means, rather than conquest, the Mesopotamian cities gained predominance over the region. "Mesopotamian influence in general spread mainly through trading and business activities rather than direct domination. This was helped by a major development in Mesopotamian society of that time, namely the finance of investment and insurance…. Such a system was superior in scope to that of neighbouring peoples whose own concepts had barely developed beyond complex barter with the indirect exchange of goods."[15]

Around this mechanism of precious metals there grew a class of men that made it its calling to control and manage this money supply, central as it was to the effectuation of cooperation and integration. These were the first merchant bankers. They could control this system because there was no internal currency, maintained as legal tender, and thus controlled autonomously by the various states. Currency was left to the market, and the merchants, together with the great estate managers, in particular the temple complexes, made grateful use of what the market provided.

---

liam H. Hallo, *Origins: The Ancient Near Eastern Background of Some Modern Western Institutions* (Leiden: E.J. Brill, 1996), p. 19.

[14]Graeber, *Debt*, p. 213.

[15]Stephanie Dalley, A. T. Reyes, David Pingree, Alison Salvesen, and Henrietta McCall, *The Legacy of Mesopotamia*, ed. Stephanie Dalley (Oxford: Oxford University Press, 1998), p. 14.

3. BABYLONIAN BANKING

Banking goes back to the origins of civilization. In fact, it is contemporaneous with civilization. For without it, money itself would not have existed, at least the form of money that developed in Mesopotamia.[16] And modern scholarship has brought to light the existence of a sophisticated banking network underlying the Sumerian and Babylonian systems of commerce and currency. A massive amount of evidence for this is provided by the clay tablets left by this civilization.[17] Tellingly, much of this material has to do with accounting, mainly borrowing and lending, credit and debt. The currency was denominated mainly in silver, but transactions were conducted mostly through bookkeeping operations. "Almost all transactions were notionally carried out in silver even if the metal itself did not change hands; and the word for silver came to mean 'money' in general, like the French 'argent'."[18] Silver and other commodities used as money base were not so much traded as kept in storage; upon this money base a great superstructure of accounting was erected whereby loans and other monetary transactions were conducted simply on the books, rather than in actual exchanges.[19]

This opened the door to what we now know as fractional-reserve banking. This practice, which follows in commodity-based banking's wake, develops where accounts on the books serve as a substitute for actual cash payment. It is but a small step from strict adherence to a 100% reserve

---

[16]Coinage, as we shall see, is not dependent upon banking. But coinage only made its appearance in the first millennium B.C., long after the heyday of Babylonia.

[17]A good summary is provided by Graeber, *Debt*, pp. 214ff. Another is contained in Steven J. Garfinkle, "Shepherds, Merchants, and Credit: Some Observations on Lending Practices in Ur III Mesopotamia," in *Journal of the Economic and Social History of the Orient* (Vol. 47, No. 1, 2004), pp. 1-30.

[18]Dally et al., *The Legacy of Mesopotamia*, p. 14.

[19]The capacity to issue checks payable to anonymous holders was another institution facilitating the growth of this credit-oriented economy: see Klaas R. Veenhof, "'Modern' Features in Old Assyrian Trade," in *Journal of the Economic and Social History of the Orient*, Vol. 40, No. 4 (1997), pp. 351ff.

Figure 1: Cuneiform tablet of the old Babylonian period (c. 1800 B.C.) with its container, printed with cylinder seals. Such were the debt contracts that formed the basis of the banking system. Source: Vorderasiatisches Museum Berlin, in Wikimedia Commons.

requirement to a fractional-reserve requirement, in which bookkeeping accounts are credited in excess of the actual amount of cash holdings. That such was practiced in Babylonia cannot absolutely be proved, for the written record does not rise to this level of commentary; but it can be implied from the results, such as the explosion of debt slavery.

The purpose of fractional-reserve banking is not to cheat the public, but to extend the money supply to foment economic growth. This type of banking system maintains a monetary standard based in the precious metals, and the restricted supply of precious metals in turn facilitates the banking system's control. Fractional-reserve banking is a virtual necessity when the money supply is based on precious metals, valued in terms of market price.

Although the purpose and motivation behind fractional-reserve banking is not to cheat, this system (and a currency based entirely upon it) places enormous power in the hands of those who control the supply of the money base. Therefore, those at the apex of the system are capable of controlling the availability of money. In the ancient world, it was the merchant bankers who could entertain the possibility of such extensive power, albeit in cooperation with and in contention with the sovereign sword-bearers.

The gains such control might afford are dizzying. By simply withdrawing specie reserves, privileged depositors could bring down banks. And if done in coordinated fashion, entire economies could be brought to their knees. Beyond this, the terms of lending could be set entirely in the favor of creditors, by restricting the issue of money substitutes and demanding repayment of loans in specie whenever the banking powers felt the need. The entire financial system, like an inverted pyramid, rested on a narrow base of precious metals. And because the supply of precious metals could never keep pace with economic growth, the tendency was always deflationary. This favored the holders of the precious metals, and the condition of those without holdings or access to them became ever more desperate. After all, there was only so much to go around.

With the expansion of the Babylonian banking regime, there came the turbulence of economic boom and bust, coupled with the unremitting misery of bankruptcy and debt slavery. In fact, the case can be made that the one was engineered in order to facilitate the other. "In ancient Babylonia, as in other ancient societies, most loans were made with objectives other than interest-generated profit in mind," writes Piotr Steinkeller. "As the extant data demonstrate clearly, the lender's primary objective in advancing loans was to get possession of either the borrower's labor or his land or often both."[20] This put the freedom of commoners under increasing threat. As Graeber notes, "By c. 2400 BC it already appears to have been

---

[20]Piotr Steinkeller, "The Ur III Period," in Raymond Westbrook and Richard Jasnow, eds., *Security for Debt in Ancient near Eastern Law* (Boston: Brill, 2001), p. 48. Garfinkle disputes this conclusion: "Shepherds, Merchants, and Credit," pp. 6ff.

common practice on the part of local officials, or wealthy merchants, to advance loans to peasants who were in financial trouble on collateral and begin to appropriate their possessions if they were unable to pay. It usually started with grain, sheep, goats, and furniture, then moved on to fields and houses, or, alternately or ultimately, family members. Servants, if any, went quickly, followed by children, wives, and in some extreme occasions, even the borrower himself. These would be reduced to debt-peons: not quite slaves, but very close to that."[21]

The Code of Hammurabi, one of the great monuments of ancient civilization, promulgated around 1780 B.C., is viewed as having had an ameliorating effect on these trends. Nevertheless, it is full of provisions establishing the institution of debt slavery as a just outcome of financial setbacks. "The effects were such that they often threatened to rip society apart," writes Graeber. "If for any reason there was a bad harvest, large proportions of the peasantry would fall into debt peonage: families would be broken up. Before long, lands lay abandoned as indebted farmers fled their homes for fear of repossession and joined semi-nomadic bands on the desert fringes of urban civilization."[22]

The long-term effect was to destabilize these societies, and during the course of the second millennium B.C., this destabilization could be seen having its effect on the nations and on the international balance of power. The great central foci in Mesopotamia and Egypt increasingly gave way to a multiplicity of powers, and the center of gravity began shifting toward the Mediterranean Sea. Additionally, the uprooted people escaping the ravages of debt slavery began coalescing in substantial fringe populations, known in the period documents as *Habiru*, which began mounting raids and full-scale attacks on established population centers.

Graeber notes that "faced with the potential for complete social breakdown, Sumerian and later Babylonian kings periodically announced general amnesties. ... Such decrees would typically declare all outstanding consumer debt null and void (commercial debts were not affected), return

---

[21]Graeber, *Debt,* p. 64.
[22]Graeber, *Debt,* p. 65.

all land to its original owners, and allow all debt-peons to return to their families. Before long, it became more or less a regular habit for kings to make such a declaration on first assuming power, and many were forced to repeat it periodically over the course of their reigns."[23]

Figure 2: The cuneiform inscription *amagi*, "freedom" or "liberty," as used in Liberty Fund publications. Source: Pierre F. Goodrich, Wikimedia Commons.

In fact, the first recorded use of the word "freedom," *amagi*, expressed in Sumerian cuneiform, refers to this release from indebtedness.[24]

The dispersion of power was facilitated by advances in technology. New metallurgical techniques allowed iron to be worked much more efficiently, enabling the manufacture of more effective and, perhaps more importantly, less expensive tools and weapons. The price of metals fell as iron tools made mining more productive, while "cheap iron democratized agriculture and industry and warfare.... Any peasant could afford an iron axe to clear fresh land for himself and iron ploughshares wherewith to break up stony ground. The common artisan could own a kit of metal tools that made him independent of the households of kings, gods, or nobles. With iron weapons a commoner could meet on more equal terms the Bronze Age knight. With them too poor and backward barbarians could challenge the armies of civilized States whose monopoly of bronze armaments had made them seem invulnerable."[25] These technological developments, combined with the breakup of the social order, spelled transformation: Bronze Age civilization began to give place to the Iron Age.[26]

---

[23]Graeber, *Debt*, p. 65.

[24]Michael Hudson, *The Lost Tradition of Biblical Debt Cancellations* (available at http://michael-hudson.com/1992/03/the-lost-tradition-of-biblical-debt-cancellations), pp. 14ff. The cuneiform inscription is also used as the "design motif" of Liberty Fund publications (see figure 2).

[25]Childe, *What Happened in History*, p. 176.

[26]A change in the form of writing likewise indicated the shift from elite to mass orientation: "It remained for the Levant, lying between the high civilizations of the great river valleys, to devise a purely syllabic script which could be mastered by the masses and which was ultimately to furnish the entire world with the advantages of a fully alphabetic script." Hallo, *Origins*, p. 35.

In the midst of this transformation, there arose a nation, called into existence precisely to stand as a witness against the Babylonian debt-slavery-based social order. As the Bible relates it, God called Abram (later Abraham) out of "Ur of the Chaldees," one of the centers of Babylonian banking, to go into Canaan and there establish a new nation: "Now the Lord had said unto Abram, Get thee out of thy country, and from thy kindred, and from thy father's house, unto a land that I will shew thee: And I will make of thee a great nation, and I will bless thee, and make thy name great; and thou shalt be a blessing" (Gen. 12:1-2, KJV). This nation founded by Abraham would come to know slavery in a peculiarly striking way, enduring centuries of bondage in Egypt before being brought out by Moses and God's "mighty hand and outstretched arm," to be given a new form of social order, central to which was a debt-release regime whereby such a condition of credit and debt manipulation would never be able to take root. For one thing, debt slavery, while provided for, was not to last longer than six years. Secondly, land could not be mortgaged for longer than six years, for every seventh was a sabbath year, in which debts were cancelled and slaves released. And every 50 years, the "trumpet of Jubilee" would sound, announcing the return of all landed property to the original owner – no permanent alienation of landed property, and thus no heaping up of real-estate holdings by means of the debt-foreclosure mechanism, was possible. The rationale was God's ownership – "Ye shall not therefore oppress one another; but thou shalt fear thy God: for I am the Lord your God.... The land shall not be sold for ever: for the land is mine; for ye are strangers and sojourners with me. And in all the land of your possession ye shall grant a redemption for the land" (Lev. 25:17, 23-24). The advantages of this legislation were:

> 1. It would prevent the accumulation of land on the part of a few to the detriment of the community at large. 2. It would render it impossible for any one to be born to absolute poverty, since every one had his hereditary land. 3. It would preclude those inequalities which are produced by extremes of riches and poverty, and which make one man domineer over another. 4. It would utterly do away with slavery. 5. It would afford a fresh opportunity to those who were reduced by adverse circumstances to begin again their career of

industry in the patrimony which they had temporarily forfeited. 6. It would periodically rectify the disorders which crept into the state in the course of time, preclude the division of the people into nobles and plebeians, and preserve the theocracy inviolate.[27]

It seems that the biblical stipulations regarding debt slavery and land tenure, along with the prohibition on interest-bearing loans to fellow Israelites, were instituted precisely to ward off the threat of Babylonian-style banking practices. In this as in all other things, Israel was to be a light to the nations.

Thus Israel formed part of the great reorientation of the nations. Phoenicia, Israel's neighbor on the Mediterranean coast, was another of these upstarts. A coastal power, Phoenicia benefitted from the shift westward to the Mediterranean Sea. It formed the center of a thriving trading network linking Mesopotamia, Egypt, and the burgeoning Aegean economy. And it forged close links with Israel during the reign of Solomon, links that would however prove deleterious over time.

Phoenicia likewise became the headquarters of the banking network hitherto centered in Babylonia. It used these financial resources not only economically but politically. Connected to this was the rise of a new power in the east, Assyria. Home-based on the upper Tigris River in northern Mesopotamia, Assyria set about establishing a hegemony over its neighbors ultimately geared at taking control of the Babylonian trading network.[28]

There was, obviously, a nefarious side to the rise of Assyrian hegemony, but it had everything to do with exploiting trade in the interest of political power. Assyria understood that trade generated prosperity and thus tax revenues, and therefore made it a policy goal to integrate and promote these trade relations in terms of its imperial hegemony. Its goal in conquering surrounding territories was to ensure that the trade networks they incor-

---

[27]Easton, M.G., *Illustrated Bible Dictionary* (New York: Harper & Brothers, Publishers, 1893), p. 395.

[28]Susan Frankenstein, "The Phoenicians in the Far West: A Function of Neo-Assyrian Imperialism," in M.T. Larsen (ed.), *Power and Propaganda: A Symposium on Ancient Empires. Mesopotamia* 7 (Copenhagen: Akademisk Forlag, 1979), pp. 269ff.

porated would be routed and maintained so as to benefit the Assyrian over-lord.[29]

But not all the nations participated in the Babylonian financial sys-tem.[30] Because Israel conspicuously stood out in this regard, the surround-ing cultures participating in the Babylonian methods undertook counter-measures to Israel's unique approach. The Phoenician connection became the conduit by which the entire Israelite constitution was undermined. The opening to this development was provided by the division of the kingdom following Solomon's reign, as the ten tribes formed an autonomous north-ern kingdom led by Jeroboam. In order to solidify his rule, Jeroboam insti-tuted another form of worship, embodied in two golden calves, to keep his subjects from going to worship in Jerusalem.

This of course greatly weakened the hold of the Mosaic legislation in the northern kingdom, opening the door to inroads from the direction of Phoenicia. As Torrey points out (referencing Micah 6:16 and 2:2) the revo-lution in legal system was initiated by Omri, captain of the army under Elah, who was elevated to the throne upon Elah's murder. His son Ahab com-pleted the work by marrying the Phoenician princess Jezebel. She in turn brought with her the Phoenician Baal worship and ensured the enforcement of Phoenician land law, as exemplified in the case of Naboth's vineyard (I Kings 21). From this point, beginning with Amos and Hosea, the prophetic opposition would ring with denunciations of the usurpation of land and oppression of the poor. "It was this constitutional change under Omri that

---

[29]Frankenstein, "The Phoenicians in the Far West," p. 271.

[30]Diakonoff argued that the nations at the western end of the Mesopotamian sphere practiced "in-kind" rather than Babylonian finance-based economics, and that therefore these economies were self-sufficient in terms of raw materials rather than requiring imports. Because of this, Assyria could not trade with them, and felt itself rather compelled to conquer them. Frankenstein disputes this analysis, arguing that, in the case of Phoenicia in particular, trade and finance were as important as they were to Assyria. But Diakonoff is on to something here: Israel's political order stood foursquare against the Babylonian system, and therefore constituted some-thing of a stumbling block to Assyrian hegemony. See I.M. Diakonoff, "The Naval Power and Trade of Tyre," in *Israel Exploration Journal*, Vol. 42, No. 3/4 (1992), pp. 168-193.

gave rise to the great prophetic movement which provides the bulk of the material in the Bible."[31]

By this means Israel became incorporated into the Phoenician and thus Assyrian system. And when the Northern Kingdom of the Ten Tribes pretended to rebel, it was crushed, never to rise again. Only Judah remained to uphold the Mosaic system.

Phoenicia for its part continued to exploit its privileged position within the Assyrian imperial framework, extending its network right across the Mediterranean Sea to Spain and into the Atlantic Ocean. This enabled it to feed the Assyrian war machine with all manner of necessary raw materials, not to mention silver, the fuel of the financial system. Indeed, they were under pressure to do so from their voracious ally, and this pressure is what pushed them to expand across the Mediterranean.[32]

Just how important, and how nefarious, the Phoenician role was during the first millennium B.C. is reflected in the condemnation pronounced upon it by the prophets Isaiah and Ezekiel. Isaiah's prophecy, contained in ch. 23, dates from the 8th century B.C., thus prior to the Babylonian captivity; it paints a picture of prosperity: "on great waters the seed of the Shihor, the harvest of the Nile, was her revenue; and she was the mart of nations.... Tyre, the crowning city, whose merchants are princes, whose traffickers are the honourable of the earth" (Isaiah 23:3,8). The book of Ezekiel devotes three chapters to the condemnation of Tyre. Here the rhetoric attains heights of intensity and vividness. Tyre is condemned not for injustices committed, nor for the abuse of its wealth, but for pride. "Because thine heart is lifted up, and thou hast said, I am a God, I sit in the seat of God, in the midst of the seas; yet thou art a man, and not God, though thou set thine heart as the heart of God: Behold, thou art wiser than Daniel; there is no secret that they can hide from thee: With thy wisdom and with thine understanding thou hast gotten thee riches, and hast gotten gold and silver into thy treasures: By thy great wisdom and by thy traffick hast thou increased thy riches, and thine heart is lifted up because of thy

---

[31]Archer Torrey, "The Land & Biblical Economics," *Land & Liberty* (July-August, 1979); available at http://www.cooperativeindividualism.org/torrey_land_and_bible.html,

[32]Frankenstein, "The Phoenicians in the Far West," p. 273.

riches" (Ezekiel 28:2-5). And for this God would bring the nations down upon Tyre and turn it into a bare rock. And when this judgement would be fulfilled, the "princes of the sea" would raise a lamentation. "Then all the princes of the sea shall come down from their thrones, and lay away their robes, and put off their broidered garments: they shall clothe themselves with trembling; they shall sit upon the ground, and shall tremble at every moment, and be astonished at thee. And they shall take up a lamentation for thee, and say to thee, How art thou destroyed, that wast inhabited of seafaring men, the renowned city, which wast strong in the sea, she and her inhabitants, which cause their terror to be on all that haunt it!" (Ez. 26:16-17). For Tyre enriched the kings of the earth, and by it were the merchants and seamen made wealthy. "And all that handle the oar, the mariners, and all the pilots of the sea, shall come down from their ships, they shall stand upon the land; And shall cause their voice to be heard against thee ... they shall take up a lamentation for thee, and lament over thee, saying, What city is like Tyrus, like the destroyed in the midst of the sea? When thy wares went forth out of the seas, thou filledst many people; thou didst enrich the kings of the earth with the multitude of thy riches and of thy merchandise" (Ez. 28:29-33).

The Assyrian-Phoenician axis would indeed come crashing down, with the rise of a revitalized Babylon and its king Nebuchadnezzar, followed by the Persians under Cyrus. These nations would subdue and conquer the entire Middle East from Egypt right across Mesopotamia, and Persia would follow these conquests up with its fateful attempt to conquer Greece. But there the conquests would end; for a new day was dawning, the wheels of history were turning, and the focus of history was shifting decisively from the East to the West.

4. COINAGE AND

THE FREEDOM OF THE CITY

The ascendancy of Persia over the nations of the Middle East signaled something altogether new in history: an acknowledgment that true religion concerned something far deeper and purer than a pantheon of materialistic, bickering gods. In Persia a new religion came to the fore, that of Zoroastrianism, essentially the acknowledgment of Light over Darkness: "It holds a position of antithesis to darkness, and this antithetical relation opens out to us the principle of activity and life;" therefore, "the principle of development begins with the history of Persia."[33]

This development was part of a massive spiritual reorientation, affecting every aspect of life from politics to religion to ethics and economics. In a famous formulation, the German philosopher Karl Jaspers spoke of this as the Axial Age. "Extraordinary events are crowded into this period. In China lived Confucius and Lao Tse, all the trends in Chinese philosophy arose, it was the era of Mo Tse, Chuang Tse and countless others. In India it was the age of the Upanishads and of Buddha; as in China, all philosophical trends, including skepticism and materialism, sophistry and nihilism, were developed. In Iran Zarathustra put forward his challenging conception of the cosmic process as a struggle between good and evil; in Palestine prophets arose: Elijah, Isaiah, Jeremiah, Deutero-Isaiah; Greece produced Homer, the philosophers Parmenides, Heraclitus, Plato, the tragic poets, Thucydides, and Archimedes. All the vast development of which these names are a mere intimation took place in these few centuries, independently and almost simultaneously in China, India, and the West."[34]

It was as if the total conquests by Babylon and then Persia had wiped the slate clean, eliminating the old national boundaries and prejudices.

---

[33]G.W.F. Hegel, *Lectures on the Philosophy of History,* trans. Ruben Alvarado (Aalten: WordBridge Publishing, 2011), p. 158.
[34]Karl Jaspers, *Way to Wisdom: An Introduction to Philosophy,* trans. Ralph Manheim (New Haven, CT: Yale University Press, 1966), pp. 99-100.

Something new was arriving on the scene, and the times were pregnant with anticipation.

The characteristic of this age, as Jaspers sees it, was a reversal in consciousness, with individual awareness and reflection eclipsing uncritical acceptance of authority and belief. "The new element in this age is that man everywhere became aware of being as a whole, of himself and his limits. He experienced the horror of the world and his own helplessness. He raised radical questions, approached the abyss in his drive for liberation and redemption. And in consciously apprehending his limits he set himself the highest aims. He experienced the absolute in the depth of selfhood and in the clarity of transcendence."[35]

The age of the gods was past; the age of man had arrived.

This shift from gods to man occurred most conspicuously in Greece. The Greeks, of course, developed a civilization in which the individual human being was placed front and center. This was evident in everything from political institutions to philosophy and art. But this elevation of the individual was accompanied by a similar elevation of a new form of social order: the *polis*, or city-state.

What is it that made the *polis* different? Although the Sumerian and Babylonian societies were built upon autonomous cities, those cities were structured in terms of great households, temples, and palaces. The social order was typically hierarchical and elitist, with only an upper crust participating in civic affairs. It is this which changed. The Greek *polis* was a much more democratic affair.

The most significant contributing factor in this democratizing tendency concerned money. The Greeks resorted to something entirely new and revolutionary in the sphere of money – *coinage*. Coinage represented a new departure because it took the standard of valuation out of the hands of private bankers controlling the bullion market, and put it into the hands of the public authority and the mint.

Much of what is written about the origin of coinage is written not in terms of history but in terms of economic theory. As the theory goes, money was introduced to conduct barter exchanges more efficiently, and

---

[35]Jaspers, *Way to Wisdom*, p. 100.

coinage was introduced simply as a more efficient form of money. It was supposedly more efficient than bullion because it did not have to be weighed and tested at every transaction. The stamp was the guarantee of weight and fineness. Or so the theory goes.

Although this is an attractive scenario, it has nothing to do with the kind of coinage established by the *polis*. In fact, coinage was introduced for an entirely different reason. What coinage constituted was a means – like the Mosaic law had been – to ward off the invasion of Babylonian financial practices and consequent creditor hegemony.

In this regard it was propitious that western Anatolia (modern Turkey) had been left out of the Assyrian sphere of influence, back when Assyria was establishing its imperial boundaries.[36] This isolation enabled them to develop autonomous institutions, one of which was coinage. It staved off foreign influence, and enabled, perhaps for the first time, the development of an indigenous, domestic market.

It appears that Lydia, a nation located in western Anatolia, and as such neglected by Assyria, was the first country to introduce coinage. Bolin has described the process involved. "At the time when the Lydian monopoly of coinage was introduced, it is clear that foreign merchants coming to Lydia with precious metal in order to buy goods would first need to change their precious metal into coins by handing over to the government the quantity of precious metal demanded in exchange for the sum required in coins. They get back their precious metal in the form of minted electrum but, on the terms indicated, only part of it. The state keeps the rest." This was because the Lydian government had discovered the true principle of coinage, which is not a government guarantee of weight and purity, but a nominal imputation of value over and above the market value of the metal used. By imposing this valuation, the government gained the difference between the market value and the nominal value of the metal brought to be minted. But this was not the only gain. Bolin continues: "In the same way

---

[36] "By the early 7th century, the Ionian and Aegean Greeks faced a massive shift of political and economic power in the Near East which effectively left them isolated and unable to reestablish contact with the now dominant Assyrians." Frankenstein, "The Phoenicians in the Far West," p. 272.

Lydian merchants who want to buy goods from foreign merchants or from other Lydian merchants must first change their precious metal into coins and so pay a contribution to the state. It can of course be maintained that the merchants need not lose anything in the exchange – they receive a smaller quantity of precious metal in the form of coins than they actually handed in, but this smaller quantity of coined metal can and ought to have the same purchasing power in relation to goods (other than precious metal) as the larger quantity of unminted precious metal handed in. This however only applies to domestic trading."[37]

Coinage thus set up a buffer between the domestic and foreign economy. In effect, foreign merchants had to pay a fee to the state to participate in the domestic economy. "If we look at the introduction of coinage from this point of view, it is trade, in this case the import trade, that has to pay for the state's profit by suffering a corresponding loss."[38]

This was the function of a fiduciary currency – a currency of nominal, imputed value, provided by the institution of legal tender. It served to insulate the domestic economy from the international economy, and thus to ward off the influence of foreign financial powers, thereby obviating the debilitating social illness of the ancient world – debt peonage and slavery.

This function of coinage was recognized at the time. The nominal form of money was used to establish a local economy centered on the individual *polis*, where the currency ran as far as the city's legal jurisdiction extended. Outside the boundaries of the legal system, that value would disappear. The fiduciary character was emphasized in the dialogue *Eryxias,* spuriously attributed to Plato but actually from an anonymous author who lived in the second or third generation after him. In the dialogue, Socrates argues that

> the Carthaginians use money of this sort. Something which is about the size of a stater is tied up in a small piece of leather: what it is, no one knows but the makers. A seal is next set upon the leather, which then passes into circulation, and he who has the largest number of

---

[37]Sture Bolin, *State and Currency in the Roman Empire to 300 A.D.* (Stockholm: Almqvist & Wiksell, 1958), p. 33.

[38]Bolin, *State and Currency in the Roman Empire to 300 A.D.,* p. 33.

such pieces is esteemed the richest and best off. And yet if any one among us had a mass of such coins he would be no wealthier than if he had so many pebbles from the mountain. At Lacedaemon, again, they use iron by weight which has been rendered useless: and he who has the greatest mass of such iron is thought to be the richest, although elsewhere it has no value. In Ethiopia engraved stones are employed, of which a Lacedaemonian could make no use. Once more, among the Nomad Scythians a man who owned the house of Polytion would not be thought richer than one who possessed Mount Lycabettus among ourselves. And clearly those things cannot all be regarded as possessions; for in some cases the possessors would appear none the richer thereby: but, as I was saying, some one of them is thought in one place to be money, and the possessors of it are the wealthy, whereas in some other place it is not money, and the ownership of it does not confer wealth; just as the standard of morals varies, and what is honourable to some men is dishonourable to others.[39]

Plato, in contemplating his ideal city-state, understood such local currency to be a buffer to regulate relations between the city and the world outside. "There follows also," wrote Plato in *The Laws*, "a law which forbids any private person to possess any gold or silver, only coin for purposes of such daily exchange as it is almost necessary for craftsmen to make use of, and all who need such things in paying wages to hirelings, whether slaves or immigrants. For these reasons we say that our people should possess coined money which is legal tender among themselves, but valueless elsewhere."[40] Such an arrangement is made possible by the institution of coinage, whereby value is imputed through the instrumentality of law, and thus holds only within the jurisdiction in which it is recognized.

Plato also recognized the existence of a "universal Hellenic coinage" based on market bullion value rather than imputed value. This was useful

---

[39]Benjamin Jowett (trans.), *The Dialogues of Plato*, vol. II (New York: Oxford University Press, 1892), p. 568.

[40]Plato, *Plato in Twelve Volumes*, Vols. 10 & 11, *The Laws*, translated by R.G. Bury (Cambridge, MA: Harvard University Press; London, William Heinemann Ltd., 1967 & 1968), p. 742a.

for "expeditions and foreign visits, as well as of embassies or any other missions necessary for the State, if there be need to send someone abroad."[41] But such money should not be allowed to circulate domestically. Such use of foreign currencies would subvert the domestic currency, which depends upon its legal-tender status to retain its value. This would subject the polity to the outside force of bullion markets and commodity-money-based banking, over which it has no control.

Thus there arose a dual monetary system within the bosom of freedom-oriented city-states of Greece. The most famous example of such a system was put into use by Sparta, with its iron coinage mocked by Plutarch.[42] However, it was not simply by weight that the original Spartan currency functioned, but by imputed value.[43]

The historical development indicates that this institution of coinage was instituted to stave off the evil effects of Babylonian banking. Graeber points out the uncanny coincidence of the Axial Age and the introduction of coinage.[44] He also exposes other similar social-disturbance situations in

---

[41]Plato, *The Laws,* p. 742a-c.

[42]"In the first place, he [Lycurgus] withdrew all gold and silver money from currency, and ordained the use of iron money only. Then to a great weight and mass of this he gave a trifling value, so that ten minas' worth required a large store-room in the house, and a yoke of cattle to transport it." Plutarch, *Plutarch's Lives,* with an English Translation by Bernadotte Perrin (Cambridge, MA: Harvard University Press; London: William Heinemann Ltd.) 1914, ch. 9, sec. 1.

[43]"To the refined mind of the ancient Greeks, it was not difficult to understand and put in practice such a system of money, and we shall find this system imitated in many of the Greek states and colonies; but to the honest Plutarch, who appeared nine or ten centuries later, and who could see nothing more in a monetary system than an uncertain and unknown number of ounces of metal to be exchanged as commodities for other commodities, the numerary system of Lycurgus was entirely incomprehensible, and, in order to deride it most effectively, he invented the silly story that it required a cart and a team of oxen to transport the most ordinary sum of the Spartan money. Like many another false thing, this story has passed current for nearly twenty centuries, perhaps for the reason that it has not been worth anybody's while to contradict it." Alexander Del Mar, *A History of Money in Ancient Countries from the Earliest Times to the Present* (London: George Bell and Sons, 1885), p. 164.

[44]"The core period of Jasper's Axial age – the lifetimes of Pythagoras, Confucius, and the Buddha – corresponds almost exactly to the period in which coinage was invented." Graeber, *Debt,* p. 224.

key polities where coinage was introduced as a solution to debt slavery. In the case of both Athens and Rome, he writes "history begins with a series of debt crises," and, "in each case, coinage became a solution."

> In brief, one might say that these conflicts over debt had two possible outcomes. The first was that the aristocrats could win, and the poor remain 'slaves of the rich' – which in practice meant that most people would end up clients of some wealthy patron. Such states were generally militarily ineffective. The second was that popular factions could prevail, institute the usual popular program of redistribution of lands and safeguards against debt peonage, thus creating the basis for a class of free farmers whose children would, in turn, be free to spend much of their time training for war. Coinage played a critical role in maintaining this kind of free peasantry – secure in their landholding, not tied to any great lord by bonds of debt.[45]

This nominal form of money, made possible by the institution of coinage, was part of the new experience of the Greek *polis*. The very word for money used by the Greeks, nomisma (νόμισμα) – from which comes "numismatics" – expresses this nominal character. "This is why it has the name 'money' (νόμισμα)," wrote Aristotle, "because it exists not by nature but by law (νόμος) as it is in our power to change it and make it useless .... There must, then, be a unit, and that fixed by agreement (for which reason it is called money); for it is this that makes all things commensurate, since all things are measured by money."[46]

Banking takes on an entirely different character under a regime of coinage. Under the Babylonian regime, it was bankers who could decisively influence the entire process of valuation, and by extension, prices. Under the regime of coinage, the state and the mint establish valuation by imputing value to the coins they mint, which will always exceed the market value of the material used (otherwise the coins would be melted back down into

---

[45]Graeber, *Debt,* p. 228.
[46]W. D. Ross (ed.), *The Works of Aristotle,* Vol. IX, *Ethica Nichomachea* (London: Oxford University Press, 1915), pp. 1133a, 1133b.

bullion). The state can only do this as long as it can maintain the legal order in which a fiduciary currency can function. Hence, fiduciary currency is a function of the legal order and cannot exist without it.

The switch from bullion to coinage confronts bankers with a different monetary environment, one in which their power is derivative, not creative. Under a regime of coinage, bankers depend on the monetary authorities to set the parameters of valuation, and they have to work within those parameters. Because the money supply – and the value of the coinage – is controlled by the monetary authorities, bankers have a much narrower scope for market manipulation and become a rather humdrum accessory of the money economy. Although they might extend the money supply through fractional-reserve mechanisms, it is by no means on the scale of the Babylonian variant, simply because control of the money base was out of their hands.

The social order was also transformed by the switch to coinage. The age of rulers and subjects gave way to the age of citizens and public servants. The regime of the citizen resulted in the transformation of slavery itself.

This transformation was the result of the mitigation of debt peonage and slavery. As citizens across the board gained a voice in the social order, the barriers of rank were broken down. As the effect of coinage undermined the power of creditors, debt slavery lost its significance as a source of slave labor. But slavery itself did not disappear – far from it. It took on a new character. The turning point can be seen in Athens, where Solon, it is said,[47] outlawed debt slavery. From that point, debt slavery has been viewed in the West with opprobrium. Testart has laid out the mentality: "What is scandalous in debt slavery is the oppression of poor or weak persons *within* a community, the oppression of those who are close, if not the closest: a

---

[47]Harris takes issue with this blanket assertion: Edward M. Harris, "Did Solon Abolish Debt Slavery?", in *The Classical Quarterly*, New Series, Vol. 52, No. 2 (2002), pp. 415-430.

relative." Contrast this with war slavery: "The meaning of war slavery is quite different. Violence between communities that are foreign to each other is one of the ordinary ills of war, as are rape and plunder; and enslaving the vanquished readily passes as civilizational progress – preferable, in any case, to killing, torturing, or sacrificing them. War slavery only came to be considered scandalous late in history."[48]

Figure 3: Athenian silver owls. Source: Classical Numismatic Group, Inc. http://www.cngcoins.com

So slavery continued its tortured existence but on a different basis: war and conquest provided the slaves that the class struggle previously yielded. The monetary system effectively changed the structure of exploitation. In the same way that it created a relatively insulated domestic economy, coinage also shifted the locus of exploitation from a domestic class struggle to enslavement of foreigners.

The age of coinage likewise introduced a new era in international relations, created by the new situation of domestic economies structured in terms of their own legal orders and their own currencies. These economies could be connected only on the basis of an internationally recognized currency, and this role was filled by the precious metals. So then, within the framework of overarching commodity-based exchange there appeared islands of coinage, spheres of exchange centered on city-state polities, expanding within that pre-existing overarching framework. Spheres of coinage thus came to constitute self-contained, internally-integrated economies. Although somewhat analogous to the large-estate-oriented household economies (as in Pharaonic Egypt), the domestic economies organized by coinage were integrated not by command and control but by voluntary exchange, property, and contract.

Within this framework, Athens pioneered a new strategy which would prove to be of decisive importance in what was to follow. In the

---

[48]Alain Testart, "The Extent and Significance of Debt Slavery," in *Revue française de sociologie*, Vol. 43, Supplement: An Annual English Selection (2002), p. 193. The distinction between intracommunitarian and extracommunitarian slavery was already anticipated in the Mosaic law.

struggle against Persia, Athens led the alliance of Greek city-states, and along with its other advantages, it had access to untold wealth, thanks to the fabled mines of Laurium in its possession. "The Divine Bounty has bestowed upon us inexhaustible mines of silver, and advantages which we enjoy above all our neighbouring cities, who never yet could discover one vein of silver ore in all their dominions."[49] This silver provided the basis for the Athenian silver owls, which became an international currency of great repute – "from Crimea to Arabia and India to Spain, the Athenian 'owls' were famous."[50]

Athens was able to lead the successful resistance to Persia, breaking its grip on the Aegean rim. But having done so, it began to impose its own form of empire upon the member cities of the confederation. One of the means by which it did so was to mandate that all members use only Athenian currency. This effort was not entirely successful, but it did show possibilities. Athens' example reverberated through this fractured world of jockeying powers, evanescent alliances and leagues, and ever-shifting equilibria. For it showed the potential of coinage as an instrument to harness the disparate elements of a geopolitical area to a common goal, and concentrate their power.

---

[49]Xenophon, "Discourse upon Improving the Revenue of the State of Athens," in Cooper et al. (translators), *The Whole Works of Xenophon* (Philadelphia: Thomas Wardle, 1845), p. 682.

[50]A.R. Burns, *Money and Monetary Policy in Early Times* (New York: Sentry Press, 1927), p. 88.

5. THE SHIRT OF NESSUS

It was left to Rome to realize the potential of coinage and harness it to the needs of an expanding state. Coinage was only one element in Rome's formula for success, but it turned out to be a crucial one. It formed the cornerstone of Rome's republican, city-oriented and freedom-oriented paradigm, over against the elitist, oligarchic, merchant-prince paradigm exemplified in its arch-rival – Carthage.

Carthage was the worthy heir of Tyre and Sidon's commercial power. It developed within the Western Mediterranean trading network, formed by the Phoenicians to fuel Assyria's imperial requirements. With the demise of the Assyrian empire and the advance of Greek colonization, Carthage assumed the leadership.[51] Carthage inherited all of the Phoenicians' gifts, talents and powers, as well as its Baal worship and child sacrifice (a horror that modern archaeology has succeeded in confirming[52]). It built up a commercial network of great importance in the Western Mediterranean, and it did so without the use of coinage. The leather "money" used in Carthage, as reported by Aeschines, probably was not a form of token currency but rather bills of exchange, in line with the Tyrian custom of Babylonian banking.[53] Carthage did not begin coining money until the late 5th century B.C. But that of course does not mean it had no money until then. Far from it.

Carthage in fact bulged with money, as it had inherited the bullion-based trading network from Tyre. But this network was coming under increasing pressure from colonizing Greeks, who tended to channel trade among themselves rather than make use of the Carthaginian network. This tendency was fostered by the use of coinage, which led economies to de-

---

[51]Susan Frankenstein, "The Phoenicians in the Far West," pp. 263-294.

[52]For more on this point, see the fascinating paper by Adrienne Mayor, "Sweating Truth in Ancient Carthage," *Princeton/Stanford Working Papers in Classics*, June 2010 (v. 1.0). Accessed at http://www.stanford.edu/dept/HPS/Mayor-SweatingTruthCarth.pdf

[53]Pace the author of *Eryxias* (p. 28 above). See Burns, *Money and Monetary Policy in Early Times*, p. 285.

velop their domestic side, and strengthened their positions within the international network.

So Carthage went to work, putting its trading partners into positions of subjection and dependency, extracting tribute from them, and forcing them to provide labor and military forces. It did this across North Africa, in Sardinia and Corsica, in Spain, and, fatefully, in Sicily – which is where it ran afoul of that up-and-coming republic on the Italian mainland, Rome.

These two rivals were polar opposites, in orientation, in makeup, in character, even in economic structure. This had been enough to avert military and economic collision. Carthage with its maritime empire did not bump up against Rome's landlocked empire, built through the conquest and assimilation of Rome's neighbors on the Italian peninsula. Only incidentally did the two encounter each other, as reflected in the first peace treaty between them, dating from 509 B.C. and stating that they stay out of each other's spheres of influence – Carthage's seagoing empire, Rome's Italian landed empire.

Rome had developed a land-based empire on principles entirely different from the Carthaginian. For centuries it engaged in war with its neighbors in a kill-or-be-killed struggle. In the end, against all odds, it gained the victory. But it used its victories to consolidate and assimilate the conquered, not subjugate and punish them. It sent its own sons out to occupy conquered lands, while also extending its laws and privileges – even citizenship (partial, not full) – to those areas it conquered. As a result, it built up a tightly-knit, compact geopolitical structure that would prove impervious to foreign occupation and conquest.

One of the main elements of this Roman structure was a bronze coinage without value outside the limits of the Roman legal order. Rome developed a domestic economy based on this fiduciary coinage, without allowing the precious metals to gain a foothold in its economic structure. This kept foreign influences from undermining the republic. When it did adopt a concurrent silver coinage, it used this coinage in trade with areas of Italy independent of its rule, mainly Greek colonies on the Adriatic and southernmost areas of Italy, and Sicily.

When it came to conflict between the two powers, it was, by and large, the citizenry of Rome versus the mercenaries of Carthage. This is a difference which has been highlighted over and over; but another major difference was the financial structure. Rome's indigenous, home-grown, base-metal currency contrasted with Carthage's cosmopolitan, precious-metal interna-tional currency. These factors taken together are what enabled Rome to withstand the mighty shock it sustained when Carthage's legendary general Hannibal invaded from Spain with his war ele-

Figure 4: Roman bronze coin, ca. 234-231 B.C. Source: Classical Numis-matics Group, Inc. http://www.cngcoins.com

phants and mercenaries from seven different lands. Carthage's ace in the hole was its mines in Spain, which yielded fabulous amounts of silver that enabled it to sustain such a war effort so far from its shores.[54] But Rome countered with its native stubbornness and resilience. By taking the war to Italy, Hannibal gambled on the collapse of the Roman framework. What he perhaps did not realize is that Rome possessed an invisible wealth the likes of which the Carthaginians could not stand up to.

> We must not be surprised to see the Carthaginians, soon after the greatest defeats, sending fresh and numerous armies again into the field; fitting out mighty fleets, and supporting, at a great expense, for many years, wars carried on by them in far-distant countries. But it must appear surprising to us that the Romans should be capable of doing the same; they whose revenues were very inconsiderable before those great conquests which subjected to them the most powerful nations; and who had no resources, either from trade, to which they were absolute strangers, or from gold or

---

[54]"The mining districts of southern Hispania alone, the regions round Cartagena and Baebelo, produced about 46 tonnes of silver a year, which was the equivalent of about 10 million *denarii*. The total cost of stationing the 60,000-strong Carthaginian army (weapons, ships, war materials, provisions, pay) at the height of mobilization just before the beginning of the war was about 9.5 million *denarii* per year, the equivalent of 44 tonnes of silver. It follows that the production by His-panic mines was sufficient to guarantee not only the maintenance of Hannibal's Italian army but also the maintenance of the troops remaining in Iberia. Any sur-plus was probably transferred to Carthage as a contribution to the overall financing of the war." Pedro Barceló, "Punic Politics, Economy and Alliances 218-201," in Dexter Hoyos (ed.), *A Companion to the Punic Wars* (Wiley-Blackwell, 2011), p. 364.

silver mines, which were very rarely found in Italy, in case there were any; and the expenses of which must, for that very reason, have swallowed up all the profit. The Romans, in the frugal and simple life they led, in their zeal for the public welfare, and their love for their country, possessed funds which were not less ready or secure than those of Carthage, but at the same time were far more honourable to their nation.[55]

Rollin's summary is passable as far as it goes; but it fails to note the keystone: the humble bronze currency. It was not as flashy as Carthage's silver but every bit as effective, and without the nefarious side effects. Which is what makes such a statement as this one by Harl so misleading: "The Roman Republic entered the First Punic War with a rudimentary currency, few fiscal institutions, and no significant reserves of precious metal."[56] This was not the disadvantage Harl makes it out to be. By evaluating the efficacy of the coinage in terms of a commodity rather than a fiduciary standard, Harl here makes the same mistake Plutarch did. Likewise it is evident that Harl is only guessing, given his use of qualifiers such as "presumably" and "would have been." Contrast this with Alexander Del Mar's assessment: "had the Romans of the Commonwealth not purposely designed to avoid the establishment of a commodity system of money, it is natural that they would have selected for their system the best instead of one of the worst materials out of which to fabricate their monetary symbols; gold or silver, instead of copper."[57] This bronze coinage was in fact a contributor rather than a hindrance to Rome's prosperity: "so long as the

---

[55]Charles Rollin, *The Ancient History of the Egyptians, Carthaginians, Assyrians, Babylonians, Medes and Persians, Macedonians and Grecians* (New York: Leavitt & Allen, 1853 [1730], vol. I, p. 158.

[56]Kenneth W. Harl, *Coinage in the Roman Economy 300 B.C. to A.D. 700* (Baltimore and London: The Johns Hopkins University Press, 1996), p. 27. Harl's lack of appreciation of Rome's bronze currency system is exemplified further in such surmises as these: "Roman soldiers presumably drew their pay in asses [the main Roman bronze coin], but even at a subsistence wage of perhaps 4 to 8 asses per month, 300,000 to 600,000 Roman pounds of coined bronze money would have been shipped to legionaries in Sicily each campaigning season."

[57]Alexander Del Mar, *A History of Money in Ancient Countries From the Earliest Times to the Present* (London: George Bell and Sons, 1885), p. 226.

Roman numerical system [i.e., bronze fiduciary coinage] was preserved intact, the state continued to increase in population and productive resources."[58] Del Mar's evaluation is superior, even though Del Mar was writing without the benefit of the great archaeological and numismatic advances that have been made since he wrote in the 19th century.

Rome defeated Carthage, but victory came at a very high price: the unraveling of the very social fabric that had made victory possible. By assimilating Carthaginian practices, Rome in many ways became what Carthage had been. Before the full course of Rome's history was run, she would manage – through great tribulation – to overcome that condition. And in the process of overcoming the debilitating effects of Carthaginian practices, Rome would produce antibodies, in the form of economic, legal, and political institutions, that future societies could use to their advantage. Building on Rome's legacy, they would be able to protect themselves from the ravages of societal disease brought on by hegemony through conquest. The vicissitudes of the Roman monetary system form a major chapter in the story of how the curse of Carthage was overcome.

After Rome conquered Carthage, it experienced an influx of precious metals, the result of war booty and a massive indemnity laid on Carthage. Furthermore, decades of Carthaginian occupation, which took place not in the cities but in the countryside, had had a devastating effect on the agriculture-based economy. This, together with the influx of booty, led to a complete transformation of the currency system. Coinage was switched from a fiduciary to a commodity basis. This was a symptom not only of economic breakdown but of the breakdown of law and order, for only through a robust legal order can a fiduciary currency be sustained. As the chaotic course of events of the following two centuries would demonstrate – leading to the demise of the republic itself – Rome's switch to a currency composed of silver and gold constituted a step backward.

But this was not uppermost in the minds of the Roman leadership, who in fact profited from the changes that were now taking place. Indeed, the wealthy landowners could become even more wealthy by taking over the derelict farmsteads and leasing the lands conquered by the state, rather

---

[58]Del Mar, *A History of Money in Ancient Countries,* p. 332.

than having those lands allocated to citizen farmers as in former days. The result was *latifundia*, large landholdings operated by slave labor gangs, together with a switch to pastureland for the raising of large herds of cattle and sheep. Both of these are of course inimical to the existence of the homestead farm upon which Rome had been built. The wealthy landowner alternatively could devote his land to vineyards and olive groves, with a similar result as far as socioeconomics is concerned. Tellingly, a Carthaginian manual for plantation owners became hugely popular, and was translated into Latin by order of the Roman Senate upon the final destruction of Carthage in A.D. 146.

The newly acquired provinces, the fruit of further victories over Rome's enemies in Eastern Europe and the Near East, provided not only vast amounts of precious metals but also a problem of administration. "After 168 B.C., the year in which Rome destroyed the only remaining great power that was within range of her, the Roman 'establishment' made the shattered Mediterranean World wait for a century before it took the first step toward reconstructing it."[59] The resulting vacuum was filled by carpetbaggers out to squeeze the subjugated countries for further gain. "The devastation of south-eastern Italy and Sicily in the Hannibalic War, and the Roman 'establishment's' subsequent policy of wrecking the rest of the Mediterranean World and then leaving it derelict, had opened up an opportunity for exploitation on the grand scale, and this opportunity had called into existence a new social class of predators in the Roman body politic." Capitalists and landowners monopolized wealth, over against the majority and the Roman state.[60]

The devastation which followed upon the wars of conquest and dominion left a void filled by speculators and profiteers. This took the form of land-grabbing, political corruption, and tax farming. "Publicans," the tax collectors, were famously put on a line with "harlots" in the New Testament. The result was an ever-expanding class struggle, together with a conflict between elites desirous of commanding the flows of wealth, even-

---

[59]Arnold J. Toynbee, *Mankind and Mother Earth: A Narrative History of the World* (Oxford: Oxford University Press, 1976), p. 258.
[60]Toynbee, *Mankind and Mother Earth*, p 267.

Figure 5: "The Death of Hercules," by Francisco de Zurbarán. Hercules being tormented by the fiery shirt of Nessus. Prado Museum, Madrid, Spain. Source: Wikimedia Commons.

tually leading to the collapse of the republic and its replacement by the Principate of Caesar Augustus. "The Roman revolution was Hannibal's posthumous revenge on Rome; but, scarifying the sinister Roman state … the deadly Carthaginian shirt of Nessus enveloped the whole of the tormented Mediterranean World."[61]

Rome was thus becoming like the worst forms of ancient empire – Tyre and Babylon combined – the message the apostle John gives his readers in chapters 17 and 18 of the Book of Revelation. But it would also har-

---

[61]Toynbee, *Mankind and Mother Earth*, p 271. The "shirt of Nessus" refers to the Greek myth in which Hercules was given a shirt on which was blood from the centaur Nessus; it burned him so much that he threw himself on a funeral pyre (see figure 5).

bor something positive – a greater, federal ideal, constituting its greatness in history.[62]

In the transformation from republic to empire under the dominion of the Caesars, Rome became something of the servant in history rather than the master. The solutions it devised to the problems of empire echoed down the ages.[63]

Rome's most significant contribution was its implementation of the rule of law. Both the concept and the content of a law of nations, where the law was recognized as standing over the state, was Rome's unique creation. It was controlled by means of the establishment of legal principles and procedures that led to a system independent of political power. The result was an independent judiciary.

Furthermore, Rome developed this legal system according to the principle of the "nature of the case." This means that judicial principles were adduced from actual conditions and relations of particular cases. Law was therefore derived not from legislation dictated from the top down, outside the concrete situation, but from this process of adjudicating cases.[64] Rome thus established the common-law principle of judge-made, or court-evolved, law as the valid approach to legal development, rather than codification.[65]

This law, *ius gentium* ("law of nations"),[66] was the indispensable counterpart to the restoration of a fiduciary currency that likewise maintained its validity across the empire. But that restoration would have to wait. For in the wake of the wars with Carthage, the currency went through major

---

[62]For more on this, see Ruben Alvarado, *A Common Law: The Law of Nations and Western Civilization* (Aalten: Pietas Press, 1999), pp. 39ff.

[63]This is a predominant theme in Alvarado, *A Common Law*.

[64]The German legal philosopher Friedrich Julius Stahl recognized this as what gives Roman law its enduring value: see his *Private Law,* trans. Ruben Alvarado (Aalten: WordBridge Publishing, 2007), pp. 194ff.

[65]Another German legal philosopher, Friedrick Karl von Savigny, recognized this character of Roman law in his famous work, *The Vocation of Our Age for Legislation and Jurisprudence,* trans. A. Hayward (London: Littlewood & Co., 1830), pp. 43ff. Regarding the term "court-evolved law," see Francis Lieber, *On Civil Liberty and Self-Government* (Philadelphia: J. P. Lippincott & Co., 1874³), pp. 210-211.

[66]For more on this *ius gentium* see Alvarado, *A Common Law*.

changes. The precious metals took their place as mainstays of the currency regime, driving bronze out of its once-important position in the circulation. Valuation switched to a commodity basis.

The civil wars also resulted in a vacuum of leadership. The various contenders in the struggles for supremacy all began minting their own coinages in order to finance their operations. One example among many: Julius Caesar's conquests in Gaul and Britain, which brought untold wealth into circulation. After finally gaining sole supremacy, Caesar's heir Octavian, who became Caesar Augustus, brought order out of chaos in both the legal and monetary systems.

The silver denarius, which had established itself over the previous two centuries as the coin of first importance, retained its place in the coinage pantheon, but Augustus added, for the first time, a gold coin to the official mix: the aureus. At the other end of the scale were the bronze issues. All in all, the new system looked like this:

a. the aureus (appr. 8 grams of pure gold); value 25 denarii

b. the denarius (3.9 grams of silver 97.5%); value 4 sestertii

c. the sestertius (appr. 27.3 grams of bronze); value 2 dupondii

d. the dupondius (appr. 13.65 grams of bronze); value 2 Asses

e. the As (appr. 10.92 grams of copper)[67]

This system, in Wassink's words, "functioned almost perfectly over two centuries,"[68] precisely by virtue of the strict control exercised over it by the Roman monetary authorities. Beginning with the reign of Nero, for example, the minting of gold and silver coins was restricted to Rome. This was one of the pillars of the fabled *Pax Romana*, immortalized in the classic words of Edward Gibbon:

---

[67] Alfred Wassink, "Inflation and Financial Policy Under the Roman Empire to the Price Edict of 301 A.D.," in *Historia: Zeitschrift für Alte Geschichte*, Bd. 40, H. 4 (1991), p. 471.

[68] Wassink, "Inflation and Financial Policy," p. 471.

If a man were called to fix the period in the history of the world, during which the condition of the human race was most happy and prosperous, he would, without hesitation, name that which elapsed from the death of Domitian to the accession of Commodus. The vast extent of the Roman empire was governed by absolute power, under the guidance of virtue and wisdom. The armies were restrained by the firm but gentle hand of four successive emperors, whose characters and authority commanded involuntary respect. The forms of the civil administration were carefully preserved by Nerva, Trajan, Hadrian, and the Antonines, who delighted in the image of liberty, and were pleased with considering themselves as the accountable ministers of the laws. Such princes deserved the honor of restoring the republic, had the Romans of their days been capable of enjoying a rational freedom.[69]

The Roman empire stood at the pinnacle of peace and prosperity. But a key element of this achievement, the stable currency system controlled by monetary authorities and protected by the established legal system, has gone unrecognized. "Its population amounted to 50 or 60 million, an enormous number by all previous standards, closely unified by a common legal framework, a network of 40,000 miles of paved roads, and a common currency. The common currency played a crucial role, providing a broadly accepted medium across the Empire and beyond for payments, as with payrolls, tax collection, trade and daily transactions."[70]

This stable currency system was itself based upon a fundamentally unstable, fluctuating supply of precious metals. And that supply had been vastly augmented by successive victories over enemy after enemy, and the subsequent looting of stored wealth. The question was, what would happen when these metals ceased to flow, when mines started to give out, when conquests ceased to bring in new stores?

---

[69]Edward Gibbon, *The Decline and Fall of the Roman Empire,* vol. I, ch. 3, pt. 2.
[70]Juan Carlos Martinez Oliva, "Monetary Integration in the Roman Empire," in Philip L. Cottrell, Gérassimos Notaras, and Gabriel Tortella (eds.), *From the Athenian Tetradrachm to the Euro: Studies in European Monetary Integration* (Aldershot and Burlington: Ashgate Publishing, 2007), p. 7.

This put succeeding emperors in an ongoing predicament. "In comparison both with the last centuries of the Roman republic and the hellenistic monarchies, the empire finds itself in a radically new situation. The end of the conquest deprives the empire, with the exception of Dacia, of the resources coming from the booty taken from the conquered .... At the same time, the expenditures on defence, administration and political activities of the empire are at best fixed, and in fact tend to rise ...."[71]

When they weren't gaining access to fresh sources of metal, such as with Trajan's conquest of Dacia, they had to make the same amount of metal go farther. And this they did, beginning with Nero, who actually devised a fairly sophisticated monetary policy, one which would be repeated over and over again during the further course of the empire.[72] The policy essentially involved incrementally reducing the fineness (metallic purity) of the coins. This policy has been denounced by modern commentators as tyrannical manipulation conducted purely for the financial gain of the ruler. Burns, for example, cannot wax vitriolic enough in his repeated denunciations. His verdict on Neronian monetary policy is categorical: "The Neronian reform marks the beginning of two centuries of inflation .... Although some of the depreciation may have been due to inadequate control of the mint or the technical inefficiency of the moneyers, by far the greater part was the result of sheer profligacy. For the next 200 years the history of policy becomes, therefore, a dissertation upon methods of currency depreciation and their respective consequences."[73]

Contrary to popular opinion, the policy was not inflationary. In fact, it was counter-deflationary. For when currency is based on metal supply, that supply has an intrinsic tendency to diminish relative to the broader economy, an inherent inability to keep up with the pace of economic growth, and thus a built-in orientation toward deflation. These conditions are favorable and welcome to creditors and other holders of money in this

---

[71]Mireille Corbier, "Coinage and Taxation: The State's Point of View, A.D. 193-337," in Alan K. Bowman, Peter Garnsey and Averil Cameron (eds.), *The Crisis of Empire, A.D. 193–337* (Cambridge University Press, 2005), p. 328.

[72]Wassink, "Inflation and Financial Policy," has a good discussion of this.

[73]Burns, *Money and Monetary Policy in Early Times,* p. 418.

form, but devastating to the larger economy. Therefore, such a policy of gradual debasement made perfect sense. The two hundred years of prosperity the Roman empire experienced under this system is the proof of its success.

And yet, cracks began showing in the facade. The reign of Marcus Aurelius was the point at which the tide began to turn. Rome went from expansion of wealth through conquest, to contraction of wealth through the absence of conquest, and the need to defend itself against poorer invaders. As outlying areas came under pressure, so did the mining activities in those areas, leading to decreasing metal production. This led to the so-called Crisis of the Third Century A.D. Authority collapsed; the imperial majesty became a football passed along through a succession of army officers. Indeed, the world seemed to be coming to an end.

Cyprian, bishop of Carthage, defended Christians against the charge of being the cause of the downturn. Nevertheless, he painted a very dark picture of the situation in A.D. 252:

> The winter rains no longer provide so much material to nourish seeds; in summer the usual heat which warms the crops is lacking. Spring no longer reaches an agreeable temperature, autumn is no longer fertile with its sprouting branches. Fewer veins of marble are wrenched from the scarred and exhausted mountains; the worked-out mines provide fewer sources of silver and gold, the meagre seams grow smaller every day. The farmer diminishes and weakens in the fields, the sailor at sea, the soldier in camp, as do integrity in court, justice at trial, harmony between friends, knowledge of the arts, discipline as a mode of life. Do you suppose that the world can be as solid as it ages as was possible when it was still young, and that it can prevail in lively youthfulness? It must diminish somewhat now the end is near and it declines towards its final setting.[74]

---

[74]Cyprian, "To Demetrianus," in Olivier Hekster, *Rome and Its Empire, AD 193-284* (Edinburgh University Press, 2008), p. 131.

The supply of precious metals diminishing, it seemed as if the world itself was winding down. Those supplies were pressured by hoarding, the mining dropoff, tribute payments to threatening tribes, and a trade deficit with the East. Successive emperors found that the former policy of debasement no longer worked as well as it had. Silver was particularly hard

Figure 6: Gold *solidus* minted under Constantine I, 327 A.D. Source: Classical Numismatic Group, Inc. http://www.cngcoins.com

hit, and as silver content approached the vanishing point, confidence in the coinage began to slip. This in turn led to unprecedented bouts of inflation in the late 3rd century, finally culminating in Diocletian's famous Price Edict of 301 A.D., decreeing fixed prices on a range of goods. The edict was a complete failure and could do nothing to stop the hemorrhaging.

The problem was structural. The empire was built on the foundation of coinage and taxation. Coinage was minted at the center and distributed by the government through its payment system, primarily the legions. Currency flowed back to the center through the system of taxation.[75] By this structure, Rome remained at the center of the world. But this was an artificial system because Rome was not the economic center of the world. It was a fiscal parasite. And when tax revenues began drying up, Rome could no longer maintain itself at the vortex.

In fact, by virtue of these hammer blows to the fiscal structure, the economy began seeking its natural center of gravity, and that center of gravity lay in the East. Perceiving this, Constantine moved his capital to Byzantium, renamed it Constantinople, and began rebuilding it as New Rome. All the monied wealth that had accumulated in the old Rome began migrating with him.

> The city which Constantine planted in 324 on the shore of
> the Bosphorus, was in reality a horde of Roman capitalists washed

---

[75]On this structure, see Keith Hopkins, "Taxes and Trade in the Roman Empire (200 B.C.-A.D. 400)," in *The Journal of Roman Studies* Vol. 70, (1980), pp. 101-125; Corbier, "Coinage and taxation: the state's point of view."

to the confines of Asia by the current of foreign exchanges; and
these emigrants carried with them, to a land of mixed Greek and
barbarian blood, their language and their customs. For many years
these monied potentates ruled their new country absolutely. All that
legislation could do for them was done. They even annexed rations
to their estates, to be supplied at the public cost, to help their children maintain their palaces. As long as prices fell, nothing availed;
the aristocracy grew poorer day by day. Their property lay generally
in land, and the same stringency which wasted Italy and Gaul operated, though perhaps less acutely, upon the Danubian peasantry also.
By the middle of the fifth century the country was exhausted and at
the mercy of the Huns.[76]

The collapse of the artificial economic structure was accompanied by
a change in the currency, from a fiduciary back to a commodity basis of
valuation. The main form of coinage became the gold *solidus,* minted at the
ratio of 72 to the pound by weight, a ratio which would remain in place for
centuries as the quintessential expression of a sound currency. This currency was thus valued in terms of its weight at the market price, not in
terms of decree. The effect was to confirm the underlying trend away from
the West toward the East.

Adams provides a cogent summary of the long-term process of shift
from West to East. "This migration of capital, which caused the rise of
Constantinople, was the true opening of the Middle Ages, for it occasioned
the gradual decline of the rural population, and thus brought about the
disintegration of the West." The decline of the rural population is the reason why the West reverted to serfdom and feudalism. The underlying pillars
of the once-prosperous agricultural economy were destroyed by imperial
successes. "Victory carried wealth to Rome, and wealth manifested its
power in a permanent police; as the attack in war gained upon the defence,
and individual resistance became impossible, transportation grew cheap and
safe, and human movement was accelerated. Then economic competition
began, and intensified as centralization advanced, telling always in favour of

[76]Brooks Adams, *The Law of Civilization and Decay: An Essay on History,* 2nd
edition (New York: Macmillan, 1897), p. 49.

the acutest intellect and the cheapest labour." Agriculture in Italy priced itself out of the market, as the lands surrounding the capital city became too expensive for ordinary farming, and could not compete with the granaries of Sicily, Egypt, and North Africa. "Soon, exchanges became permanently unfavourable, a steady drain of bullion set in to the East, and, as the outflow depleted the treasure amassed at Rome by plunder, contraction began, and with contraction came that fall of prices which first ruined, then enslaved, and finally exterminated, the native rural population of Italy."[77]

---

[77]Adams, pp. 28-29.

PART II
MEDIEVAL
MONEY

6. REORIENTATION

As Italy faded, it receded from the ranks of commercial powers. By A.D. 493, barbarians had overrun the whole civilized world west of the Adriatic. As a result, the demand for money, a prerequisite to sustain a complex society, ceased. The volume of trade contracted and gold flows to the periphery dried up. Gold accumulated at the new center of exchanges, Constantinople, bringing prosperity in its train. Hence, the collapse of the Western empire prolonged the life of the European population of the Eastern empire. In other words, New Rome owed its immediate survival to the demise of Old Rome.[78]

With the collapse of the empire in the West, gold began playing a distinctive role as elite currency, primarily to facilitate large-scale, long-distance transactions. Silver and copper currencies disappeared in the West, and local economies fell back to a subsistence orientation. Spufford asks the obvious question: "What sort of an economy was it with only a diminishing gold coinage and neither silver nor copper? With the disappearance of urban life and the shrinking of trade, the role left for the gold coinage was becoming non-commercial." As gold dried up, taxes and state payments ceased. "Without state expenditure the gold could not get back into the hands of the tax-payers. It ceased to be recycled through the economy and was fossilised in great royal hoards, which were, according to Gregory, all too often seized by rival kings with great violence and bloodshed."[79]

That hoarded wealth ran out. Rulers then began making payment in land. They divided up their realms into regions which they entrusted to chiefs, who obligated themselves and their dependents to the service and will of the ruler. Thus arose the system of *feudalism*. "The ultimate genesis of feudal organisation is thus to be found in the lack of gold in the hands of

---

[78]Adams, pp. 48-49.

[79]Peter Spufford, *Money and its Use in Medieval Europe* (Cambridge: Cambridge University Press, 1988), pp. 7ff; quotations, pp. 14, 15.

the seventh-century Frankish kings and the impossibility of continuing to pay armies with money."[80]

Economic order simplified and commerce scaled back, yielding autarkic self-sufficiency and the primacy of manorial and village life. The economic effects of these conditions were felt from the greatest to the least. Lords were not the only ones who had to make payments with their estates: petty landowners had to pay in kind or with their land, thus descending to the status of serf.

The glory of the old Roman empire was extinguished. But what was happening was much more than decline. It was total reorientation. New economic focal points were forming. The Eastern empire (centered on Constantinople) was being restricted, hemmed in on every side. A new power – Islam – swept in from the Middle East, across Africa and Mesopotamia, into Spain and Persia. In the West, tribes of barbarian Goths were taking over. The result was a totally new geopolitical power grid, with multiple centers.

The West was being reoriented around new centers, namely "Neustria" and "Austrasia,"[81] from which emerged the new primary power-holders of the age, the Franks. Alone among the Germanic tribes, the Franks had converted to the trinitarian Christianity of Roman Catholicism. This gave them a natural power base among the Christians and their episcopal hierarchy, which constituted the center of political gravity of Roman Gaul. In return, the Frankish kings sponsored the missionary efforts of the Roman church. Involvement with the church brought with it the mentality and institutions of Rome. These included the Roman law of private property and monetary payments. The church inculcated these institutions – whether consciously or unconsciously – among the newly converted populations.

But this Romanism was a thin veneer harking back to the imperial past. The reality on the ground was subsistence economy, centered on the manor. Yet the notion that this manorial economy was a bulwark of primi-

---

[80]Spufford, *Money and its Use,* p. 16.
[81]The regions of the lower Rhine and the Seine (modern day Paris, Aachen, and Mainz).

tivism that was only overcome by the superior town-oriented economy is erroneous. New research has pointed out that the manor in fact was a flexible arrangement capable of absorbing monetary ebbs and flows, and so enabling the society to maintain itself in expectations of better times.

Historians call this arrangement the bipartite manor. It was characterized by the landlord/tenant framework. Landlords combined economic and political functions. They owned the primary piece of land, called the "demesne," while tenants held subsidiary pieces. The form of tenure ranged from outright ownership to a heavily-encumbered tenancy, depending on the presence or absence of a money economy. Where money payment flourished, tenancy verged on ownership, and where money payment diminished, tenancy approached slavery.

The manor thus became the building block of a flexible economic structure. When money was short, the manor yielded the feudal system. But when money became more plentiful, the manor became engaged in marketing its surplus production. This production sustained the growth of towns and cities, as well as a state apparatus of civil servants and military. In such periods, the feudal system, with its strict hierarchy and bonds of dependence, was displaced by a social order based increasingly on freedom and equality. The Western social order thus gained the flexibility to expand and contract, with money serving as the substance engendering the ebb and flow.[82]

Here we begin to see the importance of this stage in the history of Western civilization, so often set aside with a simple reference to the "Dark Ages." For it was at this time that a new form of society, embodying unity in diversity, began developing. The sterile centralization of the Roman empire was replaced by a new approach, characterized by decentralization without entirely abandoning unity. Hence, within this new order the local community assumed its place as an essential, vibrant element of the polity, without falling into either complete, antagonistic independence or passive

---

[82]This new interpretation of the manor, emphasizing its dynamic nature, was pioneered by the Flemish historian Adriaan Verhulst. See his *The Carolingian Economy* (New York: Cambridge University Press, 2002); Adriaan Verhulst, "Economic Organisation," in *The New Cambridge Medieval History*, ed. Rosamond McKitterick (Cambridge University Press, 1995).

dependency. It was a sort of organic spontaneity, with functioning organs (local communities) sustaining the life of a growing body (the larger body politic).

These local communities were accompanied by an emphasis on the consent of constituent members. This emphasis on consent is referred to as associationalism. Contrary to the popular view of feudalism, the associational principle was most certainly involved in the formation of local communities such as manors and monasteries.

How did this work? Lords in areas where land was under cultivation offered favorable terms to peasants who would come and work the land. Under the Benedictine Rule, monasteries, the primary loci of culture, cultivation, and Christianization, were essentially voluntary associations. As the monetary economy revived, the associational principle led to the formation of towns and cities, which in turn exemplified the principle in its purest form. The strength of the associational principle depended upon the degree to which money formed part of the social order.

Hence, even during these Dark Ages the West was nurturing the seeds of a reviving economy. Resting atop the primarily local congeries of self-sufficient economies, the "high society" of the age (both political and ecclesiastical powers) maintained a thin level of exchange, mediated by the precious metals. And even during the high tide of feudalism, there were areas in which the money economy thrived. These were no more than oases within the broader landscape of economic backwardness. They were economic nodes, able to survive thanks to physical barriers and other means enabling them to shield themselves from the outbreaks of lawlessness that periodically tested Dark Age communities. And they were also sustained by their connections to civilization in the East.

At one extreme, to the south beyond the Alps, just such a node was Venice, founded on mud flats in a shallow lagoon, surrounded by just enough water to stave off attack. In fact, as the story goes, these mud flats had formed a last resort for some hundreds of refugees fleeing the onslaught of Attila the Hun; at that moment, these refugees could not in their wildest dreams have foreseen the result: a city nicknamed *La Serenissima,* "the most serene one," the queen of the Mediterranean.

At the northern end of Western Europe another center of economic activity coalesced in the region around Paris and in the Low Countries. This occurred in conjunction with the establishment of Frankish hegemony. The revived Western economy was accompanied by a new form of currency. Silver became the primary currency, and a new

Figure 7: Silver denier minted under Charlemagne. Source: Classical Numismatic Group, Inc. http://www.cngcoins.com

silver-based economy began to thrive, generating the revenues to support a new imperial agenda.

The Roman imperial inheritance was most apparent in this adherence to coinage as medium of exchange. The economy of the Carolingian empire, founded by Charlemagne (†814 A.D.), jumped forward in a new surge of commercial activity, transitioning from payment in kind to payment in coin. Trade – local, regional, and long-distance – once again came to the fore. Charlemagne revived the erstwhile Roman imperial ideal of one law, one coinage, one ruler. And he did so upon new, local foundations. His empire was less a top-down imposition than a bottom-up cooperative effort.

The renewed economic life of the West formed the basis for Charlemagne's phoenix-like imperial achievement, by historians dubbed the Carolingian Renaissance. Charlemagne for a time managed to unite France and Germany into one large political unit, and established institutions which would outlive that empire. The keynote was unity in diversity: decentralization became ensconced at the heart of Western society. This was a reflection and indeed a recognition of realities on the ground. Such an empire as the Roman empire had been, an administrative unity with a high degree of centralization, was simply unattainable, much as it might serve as an ideal. Rather than this, Charlemagne built upon the feudal system of counties – which had arisen through the need to pay warriors in land, there being no more money available – while fostering a market economy through the establishment of local markets.

In centralizing control of the money supply, Charlemagne made use of indigenous local mints anchoring local markets. "There was a rigid centralised organisation at this stage, imposed in Charlemagne's reign on top of

Figure 8: Arabic silver dirham from the Abbasid empire. Source: Yevlem, Wikimedia Commons

a tradition of multiple local outlets for coin, which had itself evolved over the previous centuries, to suit a society with intense, but very local, marketing arrangements." The legacy of this approach continued in the empire's aftermath, with a similar organization put to use in Anglo-Saxon England and Ottonian Germany.[83]

Atop this locally-oriented congeries of economies, a long-distance market order developed directed toward Venice to the south and Frisia (the Netherlands) to the north. Trade through Venice, ultimately to Byzantium and the Moslem Orient, mainly involved the slaves taken by the Franks in their incessant conquests – "The overall numbers sold were so great that the 'normal' imbalance of payments between the Latin west and the Arab and Byzantine east was temporarily reversed, and gold and silver flowed for a time into Europe."[84] The Frisians, for their part, conducted a trading network centered on Dorestad (the modern Wijk bij Duurstede). This trading network connected Neustria and Austrasia (the Seine and Lower Rhine basins) with England and Scandinavia.

With its connections eastward, Scandinavia was extremely important to this commercial empire. Pagan though it was, it provided the vital link for Christian Europe, via Russia, to the booming Abbasid empire centered on Baghdad. The trade revolved around furs and slaves on the one hand and silver coinage on the other, something which the Muslims had in abundance thanks to silver mines located mainly in Central Asia. This silver in turn facilitated trade between Scandinavia and Carolingian Europe, by means of the Frisian trading network. The silver was reminted into Carolingian deniers, providing the fuel the Carolingian economy needed.

Around A.D. 830 this commercial linkage went into abeyance, as Abbasid predominance in Baghdad collapsed. Consequently, the flow of silver dwindled. This precipitated crisis in Carolingian Europe. Infighting

---

[83]Spufford, *Money and Its Use,* p. 44.
[84]Spufford, *Money and Its Use,* p. 49.

Figure 9: The trade network linking East and West in the 9th century, connecting Constantinople (purple) and Baghdad (red) to Sweden, via Russia. Other trade routes of the eighth–eleventh centuries shown in orange. Source: "Varangian trade routes," Electionworld, Wikimedia Commons.

and civil war reared their heads. Then, like vultures to a carcass, came the marauding Vikings, themselves hit hard by the collapse of trade with the Muslim world, on the prowl for booty to fill the void.

The pressure fissured Charlemagne's empire into three parts, roughly France on one end, Germany on the other, and a swath of land running from the Netherlands through the Rhine valley to the Alps and into Italy. With imperial institutions foundering, feudalism reasserted itself with renewed vigor. The economy reverted to payment in kind and a highly local orientation.

And yet all was not lost. The manorial system retained its capacity to expand; it only needed a fresh infusion of money. And new sources of silver were indeed forthcoming to fuel the growth of a new order. The first growth spurt, extending from the mid-900s to mid-1000s, buoyed the re-emergence of a new German empire, beginning with Otto the Great (†973). Not only did Otto, who was duke of Saxony, become emperor of Germany, he even married a Byzantine princess, thus putting the seal of approval on his imperial status. All of this was thanks to the discovery of silver in the Harz mountains at Goslar in Saxony, which financed the Ottonian imperial project. But when the silver began drying up during the course of the next hundred years, that project came to grief, and Germany was divided by a militant papacy. Yet in the midst of this turbulence, a town-based commercial order had taken a large step forward, and these towns, taking advantage of the conflict between pope and emperor, expanded their influence and independence.[85]

Another burst of growth yielded the so-called Commercial Revolution of the 13th century. Behind this was the discovery and exploitation of lucrative silver mines further east in central Europe, in places like Freiberg in Meissen, Germany, and Kutná Hora in Bohemia, names which have rung through the ages for their fabled capacity to disgorge wealth. But this time it was more than an imperial project that was financed. It was a quantum leap forward in economic organization. A new age of merchant primacy was dawning.

---

[85]Henri Pirenne, *Economic and Social History of Medieval Europe*, trans. I. Clegg (New York: Harcourt, Brace and Co., 1937), p. 54.

Figure 10: The sedentary merchant: Jacob Fugger conducting business through the various branch offices shown in the background. From Schwarz's *Trachtenbuch*, Herzog-Anton-Ulrich-Museum Braunschweig. Source: Wikimedia Commons

7. FROM FEUDALISM
TO MERCANTILISM

The Commercial Revolution of the 13th century was something new, the result of attaining an economic critical mass. So writes Spufford: "As the amount of business focussed on a limited number of particular places … passed a critical mass, qualitative changes in the nature of commerce began to take place as well as merely quantitative ones." A *qualitatively* new level of economic organization developed. "This vital transformation could only take place when the concentrated supply of money, and consequently of trade, rose beyond a certain critical point." The concentration of money fomented a qualitative change in the structure of trade. "Until the critical scale of operations was reached, on any particular route, all that occurred was an increase in the volume of trade within the traditional framework. Italian merchants, for example, merely added extra mules loaded with goods to the mule-trains that accompanied them when they ventured northwards across the Alps. However, once the critical volume was reached, the scale of enterprises allowed for a division of labour."[86]

The expansion of operations and the volume of enterprises was made possible by *capital accumulation*. This positioned the merchant at the center of a new commerce-centered social order, displacing knight and priest at the apex of society. The switch from a traveling existence to a sedentary one was key here: the merchant took up a position at the center of a remote-controlled network. Influence could now be exercised through a network rather than in person because sufficient capital had been amassed in each city where business had to be done. It was the availability of this capital at every point that provided the leverage to apply force at a distance.

Like a spider at the center of his web, the merchant used his purse-strings as leading strings. "The central figure of the new system was the sedentary merchant. If you wished to be cynical, you might say that he was the arch spider who crouched low within his artful web to engulf all the

---

[86]Spufford, *Money and its Use*, p. 251.

helpless small masters and workmen who came his way. The metaphor is extreme and unfair. He was the master mind that saw a new opportunity of getting rich, if only he could extend the market and make the town grow." Regardless of his selflessness or lack thereof, the new merchant was organizing a better way of doing business, bringing prosperity for the many in its wake. "This work was done in or from his counting-house. This was the accounting house or office where the new master merchant had his account books not under his hat but on tables and well bound and labelled...." This documentary organization was one of the enabling tools of the structure, but not the only one. "Besides the books there was an iron chest containing ready cash and a balance with a set of weights to weigh the coins." This was the beating heart. And beyond these, "There were a few merchants' guides and treatises dating from the late thirteenth century. An occasional map was found upon the wall. A few samples of a new commodity might be spread out for examination. Such was the heart of the new system, the center of the new power.[87]

The merchant could only exercise this central role by specializing in money. The care and maintenance of money was his occupation. This money – clinking coin – embodied capital, and this focus on metal as capital constituted the original form of Western capitalism. Indeed, Karl Marx saw this as capitalism's very essence: "Accumulate, accumulate! That is Moses and the prophets!"[88] And his intuition was spot on. Where he and his followers went wrong was to assume that all forms of capitalism are the same. There are different forms of capitalism, depending on the type of money on which they are based. Another form of money generates another form of capitalism, a distinction that Marx never drew, nor have his followers.

This form of capitalism was based on the institution of coinage, minted from precious metals. Hard money was the indispensable ingredient in every economic transaction, a scarce commodity, having to be shepherded and guarded at every step. Therefore, while merchants needed to

---

[87]N.S.B. Gras, *Business and Capitalism: An Introduction to Business History* (New York: Augustus M. Kelley, 1971 [1939]), pp. 71-72.

[88]Karl Marx, *Capital.* Volume 1, ch. 24, "Conversion of Surplus Value into Capital," sec. 3.

have a general and cursory understanding of most things, every successful merchant majored in money. This was his specialty; trade was an accessory.

The French historian Fernand Braudel highlights the central role played by the merchant within this market economy. Merchants were not passive middlemen, nor were they the exploiting parasites described by Marx. Society welcomed the role of merchants because they served a useful function. Their central role was dictated by the exigencies of hard currency. The merchant had "ready cash, which served as his chief ally" – the scarce means which producers at one end and consumers at the other did not always have available to them at the right place and the right time. And so, "long chains of merchants took position between production and consumption, and it is surely their effectiveness that caused them to win acceptance, especially in supplying large cities."[89]

Their activity was not entirely selfless – how could it have been? Occupying positions of strength, merchants managed to accumulate amounts of wealth that gave them the whip hand in dealing with other hierarchies in society. "These men knew a thousand ways of rigging the odds in their favor .... They possessed superior knowledge, intelligence, and culture. And around about them they grabbed up everything worth taking – land, real estate, and land rents."[90]

Capital accumulation was the indispensable means to success. "The sheer size of their capital enabled capitalists to preserve their privileged position and to reserve for themselves the big international transactions of the day.... This was possible because, during that period of extremely slow transportation, wide-scale trade involved long delays in the turnover of capital; it took months and sometimes years for the money invested to return swollen with its profits." Ample accumulations were thus required simply to tide investors over during such long deferrals. This is why the merchant capitalist could not afford to specialize. He had to keep his eyes open for any profit-making venture. This was not simply to spread risk, but because no single branch of productive activity could be or even needed to

---

[89]Braudel, *Afterthoughts on Material Civilization and Capitalism* (Baltimore, MD: Johns Hopkins University Press, 1977), p. 53.
[90]Braudel, *Afterthoughts*, p. 57.

be the focus of this general, all-purpose medium. And it did not always involve profit-making in the strict sense: landownership, for example, conferred titles of privilege, and payments to princes and kings secured influence. The one specialization which did follow from the merchant capitalist position was money lending. This was an extension of the money-holding with which the merchant capitalist above all things busied himself.[91]

Being a generalist, the successful merchant was a *wholesaler*, holding himself haughtily aloof from retail trade. "As the trading community constantly renewed its structures, there seems to have been one position virtually unassailable, and which by virtue of its very impregnability was strengthened and confirmed, as divisions and subdivisions multiplied at lower levels: that of the wholesale merchant with many interests."[92] This distinction between retail and wholesale had its reflection in social status. The wholesale merchant was a new variety of aristocrat, with a position socially equivalent to nobility, while a retailer was nobody. "And the French *négociant* looked down on the shopkeeper: 'Do not call me a retailer', protests Charles Lion, a rich merchant of Honfleur, (1679): 'I am no fishmonger but a commission agent', selling on commission, therefore in the wholesale trade."[93]

The distinction ran far into the 19th century, as is seen in novels such as Anthony Trollope's *Miss Mackenzie* (1865).[94] Although it once had great

---

[91]Braudel, *Afterthoughts,* pp. 58-62.
[92]Braudel, *The Wheels of Commerce* (New York: Harper & Row, 1982), p. 381.
[93]Braudel, *The Wheels of Commerce,* p. 377.
[94]"Thomas Mackenzie, the eldest of those two sons, had engaged himself in commercial pursuits – as his wife was accustomed to say when she spoke of her husband's labours; or went into trade, and kept a shop, as was more generally asserted by those of the Mackenzie circle who were wont to speak their minds freely." So begins one of the opening paragraphs, as Trollope introduces this ticklish subject, "the actual and unvarnished truth" of which "shall now be made known." Apparently, then, the issue of this question is of some importance. "He, with his partner, made and sold oilcloth, and was possessed of premises in the New Road, over which the names of 'Rubb and Mackenzie' were posted in large letters. As you, my reader, might enter therein, and purchase a yard and a half of oilcloth, if you were so minded, I think that the free-spoken friends of the family were not far wrong." And so we may conclude that Mr. Mackenzie was a retailer. Who would care? Why, his wife, of course. She considered such a deduction slanderous.

significance, it is something we moderns are no longer aware of. Being children of egalitarian democracy, we are not cognizant of the fact that our particular form of money informs our egalitarian mindset, just as we are not aware that the hard-money capitalism of yesteryear fed into the formation of this elitist, class-oriented mindset.

The masters of monetary transactions, these merchant monied men developed a powerful influence. Accumulated capital provided not only economic but political leverage. Indeed, merchant capital played a pivotal role in one of the major transformations from the medieval to the modern world: the shift from feudal to absolute monarchy.

The wave of merchant capital that swept over the medieval world allowed absolutism to submerge the feudal order. By the 16th century, absolutism ruled the field (apart from a few exceptions such as the Dutch Republic and the Swiss Confederation). This meant that kings successfully suppressed representative assemblies, relegating them to a grudging subordination. Reliance upon the merchant class allowed monarchy to overcome feudalism's dispersal of power.

And what, exactly, is meant by "absolutism"? Absolutism was never "absolute" in the sense of an all-powerful sovereign. Rather, the sovereign was "absolute" only in the sense that he commanded the pivot point at which the various social forces could be held in balance against each other. Monarchy remained dependent upon social forces under it, and had to keep a balance between those forces in order to maintain its position. Highlighting this characteristic of absolutism, the eminent German historian Norbert Elias styled it the "royal mechanism."[95]

"Mrs Thomas Mackenzie … declared that she was calumniated, and her husband cruelly injured; and she based her assertions on the fact that 'Rubb and Mackenzie' had wholesale dealings, and that they sold their article to the trade, who re-sold it. Whether or no she was ill-treated in the matter, I will leave my readers to decide, having told them all that it is necessary for them to know, in order that a judgement may be formed." As if a judgement on such a matter needed to be formed at all! Apparently so, astonishing as it might seem to the modern reader. This is one sign of the fundamentally different mental orientation this hard-money economy produced.

[95]Norbert Elias, *Power and Civility: The Civilizing Process*, vol. 2 (New York: Pantheon Books, 1982 [1939]), pp. 161ff.

Feudal monarchy had been based on land, and the vassalage of a hierarchy of landowners. With the advance of the economy, money displaced land as power base. Monarchs then allied with merchant capitalists to gain leverage over other feudal lords and bring the warrior nobility to heel. But monarchs did not cede their positions to these merchant capitalists. They learned to play the new merchant aristocracy against the old landed aristocracy, balancing landed and monied interests in a delicate dynamic that required an adroit hand.

"The kings who, in the course of the struggles for predominance, detach themselves more and more from the rest of the warrior class as their dominions expand, also distance themselves from the other warriors through their position within the tension between the latter and the urban classes."[96] Here we see the kings occupying the pivot point between power groups. "The king or his representatives ... steers and controls this whole mechanism by pitting his weight now in one direction, now another, and his social power is so great precisely because the structural tension between the main groups in the social network is too strong to allow them to reach direct agreement in their affairs and thus to make a determined common stand against the king."[97]

The way to keep groups from combining and uniting against the monarchy was to become master distributor and controller of privileges. Western society as it emerged from the medieval, feudal order was a society characterized by privileges and immunities. This was not the rule of law but the rule of exceptions to the law. Medieval social order was based on hierarchy and subjection. Freedom was gained piecemeal, in the form of "freedoms" and "liberties," exceptions to the rule, advantages over others who did not enjoy the same privileges. This was thus the diametrical opposite of the modern social order, in which freedom and equality are the rule, subjection and inequality the exception.

Privileges had first been granted to the nobility as part and parcel of the feudal system – status positions based on warrior capacities and expressed in dominion over lands. As the merchant capitalist class moved up,

---

[96]Elias, *Power and Civility*, p. 184.
[97]Elias, *Power and Civility*, pp. 179-180.

the privileges conferred revolved around money because privileges were purchased and made available depending on the monetary needs of the prince. This provided monarchs with the funds to put down rebellious vassals, but it also ensconced the new monied class of merchants in positions of power and rendered monarchs dependent upon them. Reciprocally, it rendered these merchant princes dependent upon monarchy. In this way, everyone became a royalist; and whenever the merchant class threatened to gain too much power, monarchs went back to favoring the nobility.

Monarchy benefitted from status-group divisions, and therefore it fostered them. These divisions became crystallized in "estates," combining status and function, receiving representation in provincial and national assemblies. Such representative assemblies had little in common with modern representative bodies; they partook of the economic and social division that marked society in the age of aristocracy.

According to Stahl, the old estates system was guided by the "patrimonial-estates principle"[98] characterized across the board by the desire to preserve privileges as patrimony (hence "patrimonial estates"), without regard for the greater good. "The power of the prince and the rights of the estates, and that of each estate for itself, manifest themselves more as special privileges which have arisen accidentally, are entitled to arbitrary separate disposition, and which aim at the personal interest of the territorial prince and the concerned estates, respectively, without being related to the public condition as a higher unity, to that degree being likewise determined by a higher necessity."[99]

Such a system had been cultivated by the monarch, because his pinnacle position was only threatened when estates could unite in common cause against him. This often was a problem. When the monarch needed financial help, he could call the estates together to request funding from them. But this gave them the opportunity to band against him, as happened especially in times of princely weakness. The goal, then, was to keep such assemblies to a minimum.

---

[98]Friedrich Julius Stahl, *The Doctrine of State and the Principles of State Law*, trans. R. Alvarado (Aalten: WordBridge Publishing, 2010), p. 243.

[99]Stahl, *Doctrine of State*, p. 245.

This called for alternative sources of funding. With their accumulated wealth, merchant capitalists were allowed to purchase offices. For the crown, this became a major source of income; but it would also produce the fossilized social structure that one day would call up the French Revolution. The other means of funding was straight borrowing, whereby monarchs called on the rich and powerful – Jacques Coeur, Anton Fugger – in exchange for, in Fugger's case, control over lucrative silver mines. In this manner, certain merchant capitalists came to play a pivotal role in the early-modern *ancien régime*, underwriting the financial aspect of the royal mechanism.

It was thus through metallic currency and the institutions built around it that merchant capitalists gained a controlling interest in the nations of the West. Politically, their accumulated wealth was crucial to keeping monarchs and territorial princes afloat. Economically, their position in the center of the web of transactions made them the central figures in the early-modern social order.

Mercantilism was their philosophy. As the name implies, the mercantile interest was the central aspect. Adam Smith, in his critique of mercantilism, focused on the preoccupation with the so-called balance of payments, or money flows between countries. Mercantilist doctrine emphasized the need to maintain a favorable balance of payments, whereby money flows into the country exceed money flows out of the country. It was a preoccupation that Smith and his followers ridiculed.

Yet the mercantilist emphasis on protectionism to maintain a favorable balance of payments stemmed from the understandable, in fact imperative, desire to keep metallic currency circulating within the country. This was likewise the implicit rationale for the entire system of privilege erected by the monarchy. In a world of scarce media of exchange, economic privilege was one attempt to prevent precious metals from oozing out of the system, analogous to a system of irrigation dykes and ditches intended to maximize water retention. This was made inevitable by the system's nature. "The monetary economy of merchant capitalism differs from our own in two important respects," writes Day: "it was founded on a limited, unstable and ill distributed stock of monetary metals; it utilized the same metallic standards in domestic and in foreign trade." Metallic currency in one country could be melted down and exported to another country, where it could be reminted. In an age of scarce metals, this ebb and flow wreaked havoc on domestic economies; and "at the international level this situation gave rise to 'monetary wars' without end, every state seeking to amass specie and bullion at the expense of its neighbours."[100]

This was inevitable given the hybrid monetary system, which was neither commodity nor fiduciary but both at the same time. The fiduciary element rendered the currency dependent on the strength of the state; the commodity element guaranteed that no matter how the state tried, the currency would hemorrhage through the porous borders and threaten the economy with circulatory anemia. Hence the response, known to us as mercantilism.

When the currency has no built-in retention mechanism, mercantilism is the logical alternative. Since the fall of the Roman empire and her universal currency, the retention of precious metals was the standard preoccupation and obsession. The only alternative was a purely fiduciary currency, maintained by the laws and the power of the state. This, as in the age of Plato (when fiduciary coinage was introduced),[101] would keep the domestic economy insulated from foreign influence. Because a fiduciary currency only has value within the jurisdiction of the issuing authority, it will always return to that jurisdiction to be spent. But such a currency can only be successful when its intrinsic value falls far short of nominal value.

Every jurisdiction attempted to maintain its own currency, and one of the princes' main efforts as they consolidated power into sovereign realms was to reduce the jumble of jurisdictions, and so consolidate the currency, the better to defend it. England was the most successful at consolidating. Its common law provided the sphere of jurisdiction to give its currency national value while also successfully warding off the use of foreign currency. Other jurisdictions did not have such a grasp on monetary

---

[100]John Day, "An Outline of Money from the Middle Ages to the Industrial Revolution," in *Money and Finance in the Age of Merchant Capitalism* (London: Blackwell Publishers Ltd., 1999), p. 1.

[101]See pp. 28ff. above.

conditions and could not enforce such laws even when promulgated. The upshot was a dizzying array of coin issues.

Multiple coin issues opened the door to what modern historians have termed competitive devaluations – devaluations conducted in such a way as to encourage the importation of foreign coin in order to remint it and put it into circulation in the country conducting the devaluation.

Merchants, occupied as they were with hard currency, were positioned to take advantage of this situation. They did this through what is known as arbitrage: buying and selling metal, whether bullion or coin, on the basis of the differences in value of those metals between jurisdictions, and making a handsome profit along the way. This kind of activity was of course frowned upon by currency issuers, but it could not be eliminated; it was inherent to the situation.

Mercantilism, then, was the philosophy of this merchant-led world, laboring under the constraints imposed by the monetary system, yet also taking advantage of its opportunities. Contrary to modern notions, mercantilism was not simply state intervention against the interests of businessmen. It was the philosophy of merchant capitalists who used the state to further their own interests. They did this not simply out of selfish egotism but because they, better than anyone else, understood the exigencies of an economy conducted in terms of hard currency. Hence their focus on favorable money flows. Only with such surpluses could economic activity be conducted.

One of the major misunderstandings of mercantilism, Stadermann argues, is that instead of being characterized as the age of the rise of the merchants, the period is characterized as the age of the rise of absolute territorial lords. "Many politico-economic measures are understood to be autonomous decision of sovereign princes which at bottom were actions to promote the interest of the territorial lords' creditors." For instance, measures to promote uniform standards of production across the territory, thus breaking up local guild regulatory systems, were not imposed to benefit the prince but to facilitate merchants' marketing of goods. Further, the granting of exclusive "staple" rights to certain cities, whereby they only might engage in foreign trade, only condemned other cities to domestic trade, and had

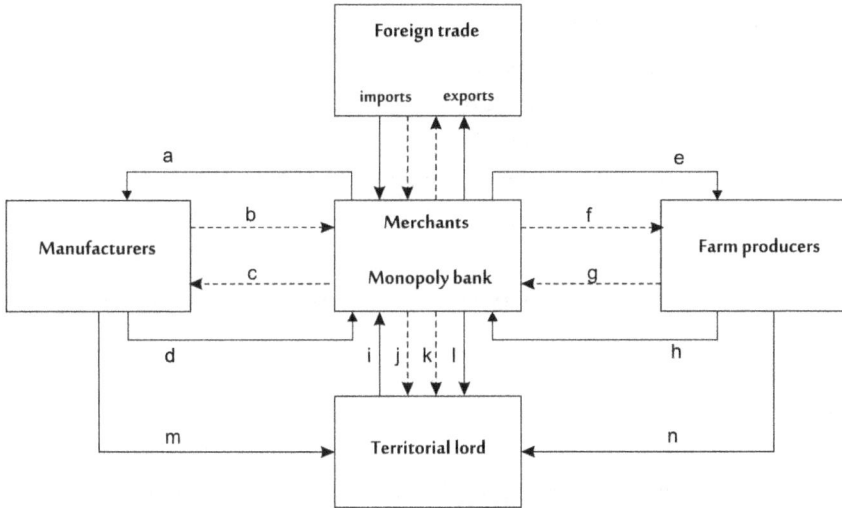

Figure 11. Mercantilist economic cycle. Adapted from Stadermann, *Economic Reason*, p. 56.

nothing to do with any benefit to the prince. And measures oppressive to trade were directed against foreign merchants, not domestic ones.[102]

The centrality of the merchant and his accumulated capital are vividly illustrated in Stadermann's schematic, presented in Figure 11. Everything flows through the merchant. The broken arrows signify goods flows, while the unbroken arrows signify money flows. The legend is as follows:

a. Payments for manufactured goods by merchants

b. Purchases of manufactured goods by merchants

c. Sales of foodstuffs to manufacturers

d. Payments for foodstuffs by manufacturers

e. Payments for foodstuffs by merchants

f. Sales of manufactured goods to farm producers

g. Purchases of foodstuffs from farm producers

h. Expenditures by farm producers

---

[102]H.J. Stadermann, *Economic Reason: Economic-Scientific Experience and Economic Politics in History* [Ökonomische Vernunft: Wirtschaftswissenschaftliche Erfahrung und Wirtschaftspolitik in der Geschichte] (Tübingen: J.C.B. Mohr (Paul Siebeck), 1987), pp. 51-53.

i. Expenditures by territorial lords

j. Purchases of foodstuffs by territorial lords

k. Purchases of manufactured goods by territorial lords

l. Tax revenues from merchants

m. Tax revenues from manufacturers

n. Tax revenues from farm producers

"Mercantilist economic policy realizes a prosperous unification when merchants take a position between the other economic actors and keep them from coming into contact with each other except through themselves, the merchants," writes Stadermann. "It is not the territorial lord but the holders of wealth who dominate the money market through the privileged monopoly bank and equally exploit both the state and the economy in protection of their privileges."[103]

The upshot of this system was the mass of privileges, exemptions, trade barriers, status barriers, hierarchies of every sort, economic, political, social, religious, all of which were tied together by the institutions of hard currency and royal (or sovereign) concession. On the surface, it appeared to be a society ruled by the nobility and the king, but appearances are deceiving. Behind these aristocracies was an aristocracy of monied wealth, surreptitiously taking control.

---

[103]Stadermann, *Economic Reason*, p. 58.

8. THE CONFLICT OF

MONETARY POLICIES

"The more there is of mine, the less there is of yours."

The historian John Day begins his article on the effects of hard currency on the Western economy with this quote from Lewis Carroll's *Alice's Adventures in Wonderland*.[104] It is a fitting epitaph over the entire period of mercantilism, when scarcities of precious metals spawned a myriad of conflicting interests that dominated the minds of men.

This mass of conflicting interests had been concealed behind a facade of pageantry and sworn allegiance to the crown. King and coin had held it all together because it was the business of the sovereign to maintain a currency that enabled the disparate conglomeration to function in a tolerable manner. But because royal expenditure depended on a limited supply of metals, that proved no easy task. In fact, over time it presented irreconcilable conflicts.

The money supply followed rhythms – "periods of relative monetary abundance … succeeded by periods of absolute penury" – based not on the needs of the economy but on the "vicissitudes of mine production." Inflationary periods followed mining booms;[105] deflationary periods, "notably the fifteenth and part of the seventeenth centuries," were "marked by the decline of precious metal production and economic activity."[106]

---

[104]Day, "An Outline of Money," pp. 1-21.

[105]"Between the twelfth and the eighteenth centuries, the inflationary and generally prosperous periods of European history are associated in turn with the cycle of German silver (c.1180-1220), then with the cycle of Bohemian silver and African gold (c.1280-1380), that of German silver and West Indian gold (c.1460-1530/40), itself tied to the great cycle of the silver mines of Peru and New Spain (c.1560-1620/50), and, finally, the cycle of Brazilian gold and Mexican silver (c.1720-1820)." Day, "An Outline of Money," p. 3.

[106]Day, "An Outline of Money," pp. 3-4.

The fluctuations in the money supply were of a magnitude that is simply unheard-of in our day and age. "There exists, in all probability, a relation of cause and effect between the boom in silver mining in Germany c. 1180-1220 and the rapid rise in prices in that same period after several centuries of a limited monetary circulation and stable prices. Conversely, a shortage of money in the latter Middle Ages was probably the decisive factor in the general decline of metallic prices." The total stock of gold and silver dropped *by half* between the first half of the 14th century and the latter half of the 15th century, due to "the continuing loss and export of the precious metals combined with the decline in mine production."[107] Although the effects of such fluctuations are difficult to comprehend, doing so helps one to understand the mercantilist obsession with money flows.

Day goes on to detail the complications involved in maintaining coinages denominated in gold, silver, and copper, minted in a multiplicity of forms by a multiplicity of agents, ranging from merely local to broad international status. Especially in the context of fluctuating supply, the temptation to devalue was great. Issuers repeatedly succumbed; but then, like penitent drunks, these same issuers carried out deflationary "reforms," restorations whereby the coinage was reminted at a higher purity. These actions whipsawed the public back and forth. "The informed public was extremely sensitive to the inflationary effects of coinage debasement, and even more to the deflationary effects of coinage reform."[108] Day's conclusion neatly summarizes the problematic nature of the age of hard currency, so different from our own:

> The monetary history of the pre-industrial age offers little to comfort the champions of economic theories that postulate the principle of long-term equilibrium. A metallic circulation, far from sanctioning, [*sic*] a certain stability, turned out in practice to be conducive to shocks and disorders that the governments of the day had the greatest difficulty in coping with, when they weren't themselves responsible because of an ill advised minting policy intended to raise

---

[107]Day, "An Outline of Money," pp. 6-7.
[108]Day, "An Outline of Money," p. 9.

the level of coinage. If, under the old regime, it was normally taxes or famine that detonated social crises, in the case of economic crises it was most often a sudden shortage of hard cash. The thesis that economic well-being depended on a plentiful money supply at least has the merit of agreeing with the experience and perceptions of an age dominated by a metallic circulation.[109]

Behind the movements of debasement and reform lay conflicting goals. Debasement was pursued by princes as the easiest way to boost their own income, and was resorted to mainly during periods of war. Debasement was an invisible tax, relatively easy to carry out and reaching all levels of the population indiscriminately. It favored the debtor and the tenant making fixed money payments. Conversely, it worked against landowners and lenders on the receiving end of fixed income payments. Hence, there was a built-in aversion to debasement on the part of the landowning nobility and the money-holding merchants.

One therefore does not have to look far to find opposition to princely debasement of the coinage. The most famous expression of this opposition was the *De Moneta,* written in the 14th century by Nicolas Oresme, who stated that such action by the prince was "an unnatural act of injustice."[110] Oresme thus had no eye to see that what these devaluations were accomplishing was simply taxation in another form. He argued that the community rather than the prince held the right to control the coinage, and that only the community, not the prince, might then act to change the coinage. Essentially, Oresme's view was that the market should determine the value of the coinage in terms of its weight. He therefore put into words

---

[109]Day, "An Outline of Money," p. 21.

[110]Oresme argued along the lines of Aristotle, that "it is natural for certain natural riches to multiply, like grains of corn ... but it is monstrous and unnatural that an unfruitful thing should bear, that a thing specifically sterile, such as money, should bear fruit and multiply of itself. Therefore when profit is made from money, not by laying it out in the purchase of natural wealth, its proper and natural use, but by changing it into itself: as changing one form of it for another, or giving one form for another, such profit is vile and unnatural." Charles Johnson (editor and translator), *The De Moneta of Nicholas Oresme and English Mint Documents* (London et al.: Thomas Nelson and Sons Ltd, 1956), p. 25.

the commodity view of money, which, expressing as it did the combined interests of landholding noble and merchant, would become increasingly predominant in the age of mercantilism.[111]

There were winners and losers in every period of inflation and deflation in Europe. The needs of war in the face of "bullion famine" compelled princes in the 15th century to resort to debasements. The interests of capitalists and landowners compelled princes to restore the currency after the need of the moment had passed. Debasements had the felicitous side effect of alleviating the scarcity of coin and benefitting those in the position of having to pay rent, "particularly the peasants," but they were "bad for the recipients, particularly the landlords." In one period piece, the *Quadriloque invectif* of Alain Chartier (1422), the peasants' purse was likened to "the cistern which has gathered and is gathering the waters and gutters of all the wealth in the kingdom," which, as Spufford remarks, was "no more than a picturesque gloss to Oresme's statement, made under similar circumstances seventy years before, that 'the devalued state of the currency has effectively cut down for them the amount they have to pay us in dues and rents amongst other things'."[112]

Regardless of the efforts of princes, the overall trend of the money supply had been deflationary. This situation changed with the massive influx of Central European silver beginning in the late 15th century, followed by the discovery of the wealth of the Americas in the 16th century (especially the vast sources of silver in Potosí, Bolivia). For one thing, the silver influx saved the English currency.

> Without pretending that the spectacular increase in the money supply was alone responsible, it is easier to understand why the curve of Spanish prices in the sixteenth century adhered so closely to the curve of imports of American silver at Seville when one bears in mind the initial shortage. As Christopher Challis shows, in a defence of the quantity of [*sic*] theory of money, it was mainly Spanish silver that kept the mint working in the second half of the

---

[111]See Spufford's remarks in *Money and its Use,* pp. 295ff.
[112]Spufford, *Money and its Use,* pp. 308-309.

sixteenth century at the time of England's own 'price revolution';
and it was also no doubt thanks to this new infusion of metal that
the currency was 'saved' from the deflationary effects of the reform
of the coinage by Elizabeth I in 1560.[113]

This sparked the "Great Inflation" of the 16th century, accompanied
by persistent devaluation. One of the consequences was the steep decline in
the fortunes of the landowning nobility in France. "The nobility who live
on the income from their estates, which they cannot increase to keep pace
with devaluation, are impoverished," writes Elias; for this nobility, the Wars
of Religion in the 16th century provided an occupation that otherwise ob-
scured the fact of their decline. "Of the economic upheavals whirling them
back and forth, those embroiled in them have scarcely an inkling. They see
that money is increasing, prices rising, but they do not understand it."[114]

The nobility thus gained an apparent reprieve from the relentless
aggrandizement of the "usurer." But, "in reality the majority of the French
nobility, on their return from this 'good' civil war, find themselves
debt-ridden and ruined once more. Life grows more expensive. Creditors,
along with rich merchants, usurers and bankers, and above all high officials,
men of the robe, clamour for repayment of the money they have lent.
Wherever they can, they possess themselves of the noble estates, and often
enough the titles too."[115] The Great Inflation precipitated the downfall of
the traditional nobility.

The silver behind the Great Inflation finally dried up, precipitating
the so-called General Crisis of the Seventeenth Century. We know this
period mainly by the Thirty Years' War. The medieval states system was
destroyed. In its place came a post-religious-war "balance of powers"
whereby "reason of state" (or naked power politics) took the helm. As a
result, religion lost its ability to restrain state power, and the church became
a state ministry of religion. The church was relegated to a cheerleading role,
corrupting her original mission of witness.

---

[113]Day, "An Outline of Money," p. 7.
[114]Elias, *Power and Civility*, pp. 188-189.
[115]Elias, *Power and Civility*, p. 189.

The new scarcity of coin also precipitated fundamental changes in the structure of the monetary system. Sovereign control of the money supply was being supplanted by the merchant monied men, who would now take over the management of its issue. With the church and her moral strictures shoved to the sidelines and control of the money supply increasingly in hand, the age of the Money Power had dawned.

PART III
COMMODITY
MONEY

9. MERCHANT BANKERS
AND COMMODITY MONEY

Merchants involved in the inner workings of currency movements and arbitrage now worked from this vantage point to assume total control of the monetary system. Merchant capitalism, once a system of trade built upon state-issued coinage (thus dependent upon the state), was transformed into a system of trade operating its own monetary system (thus freed from that dependence).

Quigley describes the process: "In the course of time ... some merchants began to shift their attention from the goods aspect of commercial interchange to the other, monetary, side of the exchange. They began to accumulate the profits of these transactions, and became increasingly concerned, not with the shipment and exchange of goods, but with the shipment and exchange of moneys."[116] The original merchant specialty now hived off into a separate class with a separate interest.

The merchant *banker* worked one side of the commercial transaction; the merchant *proper* worked the other. "In this process the attitudes and interests of these new bankers became totally opposed to those of the merchants (although few of either recognized the situation). Where the merchant had been eager for high prices and was increasingly eager for low interest rates, the banker was eager for a high value of money (that is, low prices) and high interest rates. Each was concerned to maintain or to increase the value of the half of the transaction (goods for money) with which he was directly concerned, with relative neglect of the transaction itself."[117]

The merchant banker was not a new phenomenon. Recall that in the ancient world, merchant bankers were the money providers. Although that role had been eclipsed with the advent of coinage, it now reemerged on the age-old foundation of banker supremacy: commodity money.

---

[116]Carroll Quigley, *Tragedy and Hope: A History of the World in Our Time* (New York: Macmillan, 1966), p. 45.

[117]Quigley, *Tragedy and Hope*, p. 45.

Merchant bankers worked tirelessly to remove from princes or other public authorities the power to manage currencies. They did this by pushing currencies on a commodity basis. In such a system, the state certainly still had a role to play. It declared the metal of which the currency was to be composed, along with its fineness, size, shape, etc. But that was all there was to legal tender. Quantity was left to the "marketplace." In this manner the regime of *free coinage* was established.

The Bank of Amsterdam led the way. It received all currencies without restriction. This in itself drew currencies of all shapes and sizes to the coffers of the Bank, where they were deposited. Trade was conducted on the basis of clearinghouse activities – transactions being settled internally, inside the bank, between the accounts of depositors.

Holland's concentration of currency, both the result of and a stimulus to trading activity, drew upon it the opprobrium of other nations. This led to the country's being invaded in 1672 by Louis XIV, backed by England's Charles II. One of the *casus belli* was indeed French finance minister Colbert's envy of the Dutch primacy in world trade, as embodied in the Bank of Amsterdam. A subject of constant discussion and complaint was the favorable state of Dutch finances, the result of the attraction of capital, leading to low interest rates and economic growth. The pull on currency exerted by the Dutch *entrepôt* drained the other nations of specie, much to their rulers' irritation.

Currencies were attracted to Holland by its position as the pivot in a burgeoning world economy. Trade to the East, which in the 17th century centered in Amsterdam, could only be conducted on the basis of vast sums of silver to offset the trade imbalance. Dutch policy flew in the face of received wisdom: the Dutch opened the doors to the free import and export of currency. It was a policy that yielded it the requisite silver to conduct the eastward trade. Holland was awash in currency to finance trade in all directions. This was the mirror image of the rest of Europe, which faced a dearth of currency.[118]

---

[118]The influx of currency also fueled the famed Tulip Mania of the 1630s. See Doug French, "The Dutch Monetary Environment During Tulipmania," in *The Quarterly Journal of Austrian Economics* (Vol. 9, No. 1, Spring 2006), pp. 3-14.

Besides Colbert's approach, there was the English one: rather than combat Amsterdam, copy it. The merchant bankers of England, following the example of the Bank of Amsterdam, now switched to a different strategy by which the metallic coinage was thrown open to pure market forces. The path was opened to this by Charles II, when he allowed bullion to be exported (1662)[119] and when he commanded the mints to coin all precious metals free of charge (1666).[120]

Free coinage entails the unrestricted access of bullion holders to the mint: anyone with coinable gold and/or silver could bring that metal to the mint to obtain the equivalent, in weight, in coins. The establishment of free coinage removes control of the money supply from the hands of the sovereign and places it in the hands of market forces.

At first this might seem a good thing; after all, was it not selfishness and greed that actuated the monetary policy of princes? Would not market forces now take charge? In reality, this money market was not an open one, flush with liquidity. It was the restricted domain of merchant bankers, a closed group jealously guarding that arcane world they had spent centuries developing. In fact, the establishment of free coinage might well be seen as an instance of Brer Rabbit begging not to be thrown into the briar patch.[121]

---

[119]See page 87 below.

[120]*Statutes*, 18 *Chas.* II, 5, 1666: "Whereas it is most obvious that the plenty of current coins of gold and silver of this kingdom is of great advantage to trade and commerce . . . be it enacted . . that whatsoever person or persons, native or foreigner, alien or stranger, shall from and after the twentieth day of December one thousand six hundred sixty and six, bring in any foreign coin, plate or bullion of gold or silver, in mass, molten or alloyed, or any sort of manufacture of gold or silver, into his Majesty's mint or mints within the kingdom of England, to be there melted down and coined into the current coins of this kingdom, shall have the same there assayed, melted down and coined with all convenient speed, without any defalcation, diminution or charge for the assaying, coinage or waste in coinage: so as that for every pound troy of crown or standard gold that shall be brought in and delivered by him or them . . . there shall be delivered ... a pound troy of the current coins of this kingdom, of crown or standard gold." From *English Economic History: Selected Documents,* compiled and edited by A.E. Bland, P.A. Brown, and R.H. Tawney (London: G. Bell and Sons, Ltd, 1914), pp. 674-675.

[121]"Den Brer Rabbit talk mighty 'umble. 'I don't keer w'at you do wid me, Brer Fox,' sezee, 'so you don't fling me in dat brier-patch. Roas' me, Brer Fox,' sezee, 'but don't fling me in dat brier-patch,' sezee. 'Hit's so much trouble fer ter

It might seem that delivering the money supply over to market forces would take it out of the hands of any particular set of individuals, in particular the state. But the very nature of the bullion- and coinage-based money supply lent itself to being "cornered," and the merchant banking community was admirably positioned to bring this about. In this light, the wish of Mirabeau, expressed during the deliberations of the French National Assembly in 1790, becomes comprehensible: "A money dependent neither upon the fertility of the mines, nor upon the avarice nor caprice of their possessors."[122]

The key reason for seeking to gain control of the currency markets was to conduct the lucrative trade with the East, with its voracious appetite for silver. The merchant bankers of London, enabled by the allowance to export bullion and currency, could now conduct that trade. For without command of currency – silver – they would not have the wherewithal to do so. For this reason, the East India Company was the major institutional force behind the change in monetary policy.

But this interest required the sacrifice of domestic interests. The favor now found by the East India Company (bribing members of Parlia-

---

kindle a fier,' sez Brer Fox, sezee, 'dat I speck I'll hatter hang you,' sezee. 'Hang me des ez high as you please. Brer Fox,' sez Brer Rabbit, sezee, 'but do fer de Lord's sake don't fling me in dat brier-patch,' sezee. 'I ain't got no string,' sez Brer Fox, sezee, 'en now I speck I'll hatter drown you,' sezee. 'Drown me des ez deep ez you please, Brer Fox,' sez Brer Rabbit, sezee, 'but do don't fling me in dat brier-patch,' sezee. 'Dey ain't no water nigh,' sez Brer Fox, sezee, 'en now I speck I'll hatter skin you,' sezee. 'Skin me, Brer Fox,' sez Brer Rabbit, sezee, 'snatch out my eyeballs, t'ar out my years by de roots, en cut off my legs,' sezee, 'but do please, Brer Fox, don't fling me in dat brier-patch,' sezee. Co'se Brer Fox wanter hurt Brer Rabbit bad ez he kin, so he cotch 'im by de behime legs en slung 'im right in de middle er de brier-patch. Dar wuz a considerbul flutter whar Brer Rabbit struck de bushes, en Brer Fox sorter hang 'roun' for ter see w'at wuz gwineter happen. Bimeby he hear somebody call 'im en way up de hill he see Brer Rabbit settin' cross-legged on a chinkapin log, koamin' de pitch outen his har wid a chip. Den Brer Fox know dat he bin swop off mighty bad. Brer Rabbit wuz bleedzed for ter fling back some er his sass, en he holler out: 'Bred en bawn in a brier-patch. Brer Fox – bred en bawn in a brier-patch!' en wid dat he skip out des ez lively ez a cricket in de embers." Joel Chandler Harris, *Uncle Remus: Or, Mr. Fox, Mr. Rabbit, and Mr. Terrapin* (London: George Routledge and Sons, Ltd, 1883), pp. 16-18.

[122]Quoted in Del Mar, *Money and Civilization*, p. 292.

ment as it went along) was not shared by those who experienced the negative side-effects of money shortages brought about by the silver export to feed the East. These shortages especially disadvantaged the "common run," not the elite. The interests of the nation were being sacrificed to the profits of merchants and bankers.

In the House of Lords, the bill removing restrictions on precious metal exports attracted vehement protest. The Earl of Anglesey, Arthur Annesley, on 24 July 1663 launched a scathing attack upon it. In the first place, he argued, the bill "crosseth the wisdom and care of our ancestors of all ages, who by many laws and penalties, upon excellent and approved grounds, have restrained such exportation, and thereby preserved trade in a flourishing condition." In other words, it contradicted the mercantilist doctrine to restrict currency flows. For, "there appearing already great want of money in his Majesty's dominions, and almost all the gold of his Majesty's stamp gone, notwithstanding the restraint laid by law, and the importation of foreign commodities (which are grown to so great an esteem and use amongst us) being much greater than the export of our native and simple commodities, it must necessarily follow, by this free exportation, that our silver will also be carried away into foreign parts, and all trade fail for want of money, which is the measure of it." Furthermore, the country will suffer from a lack of specie to conduct domestic trade, but also a dropoff in foreign trade, because merchants will prefer to ship silver than goods, upon which they have to pay custom. The worst of it is the removal of the royal prerogative, now placed firmly in the hands of private parties. Outlines of the Money Power can be clearly delineated: "It trencheth highly upon the King's prerogative, he being by the law the only exchanger of money, and his interest equal to command that as to command the militia of the kingdom, which cannot subsist without it; and *it is dangerous to the peace of the kingdom, when it shall be in the power of half a dozen or half a score rich, discontented, or factious persons, to make a bank of our coin and bullion beyond the seas for any mischief, and leave us in want of money.*"[123] Truly a prophetic glimpse into the future!

This was the complaint in 1663, during the reign of the Catholic-leaning House of Stuart; but the situation did not change with the switch in 1689 to the Protestant House of Orange. The accession of William III to the throne made sure of that, because William was beholden to the interests behind the shift toward currency-market control. After all, the merchants in Amsterdam, who bankrolled William's campaign to assume the throne in England, were keen to get in on the action in London. In fact, an international banking "syndicate" was now being formed, the better to maintain currency control and trade hegemony.

One of the consequences was the so-called Great Recoinage of 1695. Having taken notice of the atrocious state of the silver currency, afflicted by a dearth whereby only the poorest exemplars still circulated, the crown, listening to "experts" like the renowned philosopher John Locke, ordered the silver coinage to be restored to its mint value at the time of Elizabeth I. However, because this mint value in fact left the coinage undervalued vis-a-vis the bullion market, "the recoinage of 1696 was accomplished on a ratio basis which left the English coinage exposed for many a long year to just the same evils of arbitrage operations which had reduced it previously to so extraordinary and deplorable a state of depreciation."[124] The recoined silver promptly disappeared from circulation, thus doing nothing to alleviate the condition of currency scarcity. With the Royal Mint pursuing a policy which for all practical purposes established gold over silver, gold flowed into the country while silver flowed out, which was of great value to the East India trade but detrimental to the country at large, as it caused continued specie shortages.

So how did England manage to become the economic power that it did during this period? By means of a truly remarkable innovation. This was

---

[123] *The History and Proceedings of the House of Lords from the Restoration in 1660 to the Present Time: Containing the Most Remarkable Motions, Speeches, Debates, Orders and Resolutions, Volume the First, from 1660, to 1697* (London: Printed for Ebenezer Timberland, 1742), pp. 65-66. Italics added.

[124] Wm. A. Shaw, *Select Tracts and Documents Illustrative of English Monetary History 1626-1730* (London: Clement Wilson, 1896), p. 122.

the Bank of England, established during this same period, in 1694, as a body chartered to lend money to the government, in exchange for which it was granted the authority to issue bank notes.

The "Bank's" bank notes filled part of the void left by the shortage of currency, although available only to the well-to-do. These bank notes were redeemable – that is, they were convertible into specie – but in practice this did not occur often. As a result, actual bank reserves fell far short of the amount of bank notes outstanding. Thus, the Bank of England became the first official reserve bank of modern times, setting a far-reaching precedent.

Although precedent-setting, these banking policies were anything but new. The Bank of England had returned to the Babylonian commodity-based practice of ancient times. As the mechanism of coinage was dismantled, the Carthaginian shirt of Nessus was awaiting its new bearer.

10. SILVER AND GOLD

Silver and gold, silver and gold
Ev'ryone wishes for silver and gold
How do you measure its worth?
Just by the pleasure it gives here on earth.[125]

Consciously or unconsciously, by undervaluing silver against gold England was putting itself on a gold standard, over against the other European countries, that for their part maintained a bimetallic system of gold and silver.

Gold had been the cornerstone of the Roman currency system, both before the collapse of the West and after. The eastern Empire had continued an illustrious existence, and gold was one of its enduring legacies. Constantinople being the center of the empire both politically and economically, gold flowed to it and through it. Its gold coin, known in the West as the bezant by virtue of its origin (Byzantium), was, in Robert Lopez's pregnant phrase, the "dollar of the Middle Ages."[126] The bezant was the empire's claim to fame. It was universally recognized as the currency of choice for international trade. For centuries it was maintained at the same high standard of purity – Constantine's original ratio of 72 *solidi* to the ounce – a system that for the most part enabled the state to cover its outlays with tax revenues and state-owned mines.

But Islam's conquest of the Levant, Egypt, and North Africa removed the empire's wealthiest regions from its control and also cut off one of its major sources of gold – Nubia along the upper Nile. Henceforth, gold had to be acquired via a favorable balance of trade, and mercantilist policies were the order of the day, throttling economic growth. The question is whether Byzantium would have been better off with a "looser" monetary policy, one allowing for expansion rather than stability. Lopez points to the

---

[125]From "Silver and Gold," sung by Burl Ives, written by Johnny Marks. Lyrics copyright St. Nicholas Music Inc.

[126]Robert S. Lopez, "The Dollar of the Middle Ages," in *The Journal of Economic History*, Vol. 11, No. 3, Part 1 (Summer, 1951), pp. 209-234.

Figure 12: The 'dollar' of the Middle Ages. Byzantine *solidus* or "bezant," minted under Constantine VIII. Source: Wikimedia Commons.

lack of credit facilities and other commercial institutions putting Byzantium at a competitive disadvantage with the countries of Islam and, increasingly, the West. The Byzantine state policy was rigid and unmoved by merchant considerations.

The empire that amazed the world by the profusion of its riches and by the abundance of its gold coinage was constantly threatened with exhaustion of its stock of precious metals. This fact, which has escaped the attention of modern critics of Byzantium, goes a long way toward explaining the conservatism and sometimes the stinginess of the administration as well as the reluctance of the merchants to venture large investments and to meet foreign traders in foreign markets rather than in the protected hothouses of the supervised buildings and fairs of the empire. Still, this defensive attitude was an obstacle to expansion of the foreign trade that alone could have attracted larger currents of gold. Perhaps the vicious circle could have been broken if a monetary inflation or an expansion of credit had stimulated home production and enabled the Byzantine merchants to flood foreign markets with cheaper goods; but the bezant remained stable and credit did not grow.[127]

Gold became an albatross around the empire's neck; the single-minded pursuit of coined perfection contributed in great degree to the empire's demise, for when it did finally resort to debasement, it was as if the dam broke: "The metal content of the *hyperpyron* [the successor coin to the bezant] lost all stability and went rapidly downhill."[128] The downward trend turned precipitous; confidence waned, turning to despair.

When Byzantium finally fell, it was not so much Islam – although, of course, the *coup de grâce* was administered by the Turks in 1453 – but the

---

[127]Lopez, "The Dollar of the Middle Ages," p. 228.

[128]Marc Bloch, "The Problem of Gold in the Middle Ages," in *Land and Work in Mediaeval Europe: Selected Papers by Marc Bloch*, trans. J.E. Anderson (London: Routledge and Kegan Paul, 1967), p. 211.

Latins of the West that did it. This, not the ephemeral establishment of feudal kingdoms in the Levant, was the major legacy of the Crusades. The hammer blows from land and sea administered by the Latins loosened Byzantium's grip on its seagoing trade empire. Hegemony over that Mediterranean empire – the dubious Carthaginian legacy – now fell to the Italian city-states, primarily Venice, which, with the gold now flowing into its coffers

Figure 13: Venetian ducat, minted under Doge Michele Steno (1400-1413). Source: Classical Numismatic Group, Inc. http://www.cngcoins.com

rather than Constantinople's, began minting its famed ducats. Beginning in the 14th century, the ducat became the new standard of international commerce.

But this gold came with a price: the requirement to maintain a favorable balance of payments, or, in other words, to sell enough other things with which to buy the gold. And one of those "other things" was silver, which in the West was relatively abundant. In the East, silver was in great demand while gold was relatively abundant. Thus, where the balance of trade fell short, the shortfall could be made up with silver.

The Crusades formed the turning point not only in the fortunes of Byzantium, but also in the flow of precious metals. The Latins brought with them the silver which was relatively plentiful in the West and lacking in the East. This was one of the advantages that enabled them to maintain themselves in their precarious position. They exchanged silver for gold and began minting their own gold coinages, in enough quantities to undermine the bezant. "The Latin kingdoms were therefore a point of leverage around which the monetary history of both East and West turned. Through them the East obtained the silver which brought the silver famine to an end. And in these kingdoms Europeans again began minting gold, drew considerable supplies of gold out of the neighbouring countries, and undermined what had been the strongest gold currency in the world."[129] The resultant collapse of Byzantium opened the way for the Italian city-states, particularly

---

[129] Alan M. Watson, "Back to Gold – and Silver," in *The Economic History Review* (Second Series, Volume XX, No. 1, 1967), p. 11.

Figure 14: The Venetian-led Fourth Crusade of 1204, not against the Muslims, but against Christian Constantinople: "The Taking of Constantinople" by Palma Le Jeune. Source: Wikimedia Commons.

Venice.

From this point, the kingdoms of Europe began to pursue gold coinages at the expense of silver. The consequences for the countries at large were grave: "Rulers in all parts of Europe were ready to procure the metal needed to maintain a strong gold currency by sacrificing silver. They were prepared to let the common people, who received their incomes in silver, bear the burden of keeping intact a prestige coinage for the use of princes and merchants."[130]

And that burden was heavy. "Almost as soon as gold was minted in a region, difficulties were experienced in maintaining a silver coinage, and shortages often became acute. To guard against the loss of silver, laws were

---

[130]Watson, "Back to Gold," p. 33.

passed in most parts of Europe forbidding the export of coins and unminted metals. That these laws ... were not successful is evident. Almost everywhere the coming of gold enfeebled silver."[131]

Making matters worse, the silver mines of Central Europe, from which had come the metal to sustain the Commercial Revolution of the 13th century, were drying up. "Through the thirteenth century great finds of silver at Freiberg, Iglau and Kutná Hora had succeeded each other, so that, when one group of mines began to be exhausted, another took over. After the Kutná Hora mines, however, there was no major new discovery of silver until the 1460s."[132]

So the campaign for gold could not have come at a worse time. But this did not hinder the merchants involved in the bullion trade from exporting silver. They were only taking advantage of the favorable exchange rate. But merchants were risking the displeasure of rulers, who were becoming aware of the negative consequences – impoverishment and tumultuous unrest. No one, not even the great Jacques Coeur, the 15th century financier of the French crown, was safe from royal legislation against silver bullion export. "In vain did Coeur plead that 'ce n'estoit pas grant mal de la faire hors du Royaume' [It is no great evil to the kingdom] and that 'pour chacun marc d'argent a fait venir ung marc d'or au Royaume" [for every mark of silver, a mark of gold returns to the kingdom].[133] The reason for taking such great risks with the law? "Il a prouffit a porter argent blanc en Suyrie, car quand il vault 6 escus par deca il en vault 7 par dela" [It is profitable to carry silver to Syria, when it is worth 6 ecus here, it is worth 7 ecus there].[134]

The export of silver in favor of gold, while beneficial to certain commercial interests, was destroying the fabric of society, because gold was used by only a few, while silver was the major currency for everyday transactions. "It is clear that even highly skilled craftsmen, let alone the ordinary run of men, hardly ever used gold coins, and that most men in the fifteenth century never handled gold coins at all. For most men, however, silver

---

[131]Watson, "Back to Gold," p. 32.
[132]Spufford, *Money and Its Use,* p. 343.
[133]Watson, "Back to Gold," p. 21.
[134]Quoted in Watson, "Back to Gold," p. 21.

coins were much more important, and the key silver coins that had evolved by the early fifteenth century were of a value that was useful for the major payments of everyday life – wages, rents, taxes."[135] This, along with the need to finance ever-recurring wars, in particular the Hundred Years' War between the French and English crowns, led to what Spufford referred to as "the scourge of debasement," with silver steadily reduced in quality and weight to the point that, for years on end, mints ceased activity altogether.

The attempt to reinstate gold as the cornerstone of the money supply thus foundered. Society was saved by the discovery of new sources of silver, made accessible by new technology.[136] When the new silver mines in eastern Europe came on line, succeeded by the fabulous silver mines of Mexico and Peru, there followed the Great Inflation.

Regarding this fortuitous turn of events, Alison penned these once-famous though now-forgotten lines:

> The two greatest events which have occurred in the history of mankind have been directly brought about by a successive contraction and expansion of the circulating medium of society. The fall of the Roman Empire, so long ascribed, in ignorance, to slavery, heathenism, and moral corruption, was in reality brought about by a decline in the gold and silver mines of Spain and Greece, from which the precious metals for the circulation of the world were drawn, at the very time when the victories of the legions, and the wisdom of the Antonines, had given peace and security, and, with it, an increase in numbers and riches to the Roman Empire. This growing disproportion, which all the efforts of man to obviate its effects only tended to aggravate, coupled with the simultaneous importation of grain from Egypt and Libya at prices below what it could be

---

[135]Spufford, *Money and Its Use,* p. 323.

[136]Two advances in particular paved the way for the resurgence of silver mining: horse- and water-powered drainage pumps, enabling mining shafts to go much deeper, and the *Saigerhütten* smelting process, providing a hotter flame by which silver could be more effectively extracted from ore. See John H. Munro, "South German silver, European textiles, and Venetian trade with the Levant and Ottoman Empire, c.1370 to c.1720: a Non-mercantilist Approach to the Balance of Payments Problem," in *Relazione Economiche tra Europa e Mondo Islamico, Seccoli XIII-XVIII,* ed. Simonetta Cavaciocchi (Florence, 2006), pp. 910-911.

Figure 15: "When [Columbus] spread his sails across the Atlantic, he bore mankind and its fortunes in his bark." Christopher Columbus arrives in America. Source: L. Prang & Co., Wikimedia Commons.

raised at in the Italian fields, produced that constant decay of agriculture and rural population, and increase in the weight of debts and taxes, to which all the contemporary annalists ascribe the ruin of the Empire. And as if Providence had intended to reveal in the clearest manner the influence of this mighty agent on human affairs, the resurrection of mankind from the ruin which these causes had produced was owing to the directly opposite set of agencies being put in operation. Columbus led the way in the career of renovation; when he spread his sails across the Atlantic, he bore mankind and its fortunes in his bark. The mines of Mexico and Peru were opened to European enterprise: the real riches of those regions were augmented by fabulous invention; and the fancied El Dorada of the New World attracted the enterprising and ambitious from every country to its shores. Vast numbers of the European, as well as the Indian race, perished in the perilous attempt, but the ends of Nature were accomplished. The annual supply of the precious metals for the use of the globe was tripled; before a century had expired, the prices of every species of produce were quadrupled. The weight of

debt and taxes insensibly wore off under the influence of that prodigious increase in the renovation of industry; the relations of society
were changed; the weight of feudalism cast off; the rights of man
established. Among the many concurring causes which conspired to
bring about this mighty consummation, the most important, though
hitherto the least observed, was the discovery of the mines of Mexico and Peru.[137]

Silver was indeed back, and with a vengeance. In fact, it was the key
element in the formation of the first truly global trading order. That might
seem odd, considering that silver was never the currency of international
trade the way gold was. But it was not as an international currency that
silver served to engender a world trading order. Rather, it was as an object
of domestic demand. This demand for silver in the Far East, matched with
the supply of silver from Europe and the Americas, provided the crucial
element in establishing a global trading order. But in the end this led to the
re-establishment of the primacy, indeed domination, of gold over the trading nations.

The center of this new silver-based world order was China. At first
sight this would seem strange, what with China's image as an inward-look-
ing, self-sufficient empire. But China's domestic economy had switched
from a paper-based to a silver-based currency, with silver being valued in
terms of a commodity rather than a fiduciary standard. The switch was
made precisely because the Chinese state could no longer maintain its
centuries-long tradition of fiduciary currency, consisting of paper money
and bronze coinage.

"In contrast to European and West Asian states," writes Von Glahn,
"the Chinese empire never coined precious metals; instead, its monetary
system was predicated on bronze coin. Yet the state's inability to produce
sufficient quantities of bronze coin prompted the use of other base metals,
such as iron, in coinage and also led to the introduction of paper currency
in the eleventh century."[138] The state eventually lost control of this system,

[137]Sir Archibald Alison, *History of Europe from the Fall of Napoleon in MDCCCXV to the Accession of Louis Napoleon in MDCCCLII* (Edinburgh and London: William Blackwood and Sons, 1852), pp. 29-30.
[138]Richard von Glahn, "Myth and Reality of China's Seventeenth-Century

forcing its hand. "Private commerce burgeoned while the autocratic state could no longer wield control of its instrument, the bronze coin. Government-backed plans proposed during the sixteenth century by various statesmen to create a balanced multiple currency system with fixed rations [sic] of exchange came to nothing. Regional monetary systems defied these attempts at standardization, and the government inevitably had no choice but to accept silver in the payment of taxes."[139]

With China acting as a "suction pump"[140] for silver, world demand for it skyrocketed, and the vortex of that demand was firmly located in China: "The premium silver obtained in China made the Chinese market the final destination of world-wide silver flows. Thus the retired Portuguese merchant Gomes Solis could write in his *Arbitrio sobre la plata*, published in Lisbon in 1621, that 'silver wanders throughout all the world in its peregrinations before flocking to China, where it remains, as if at its natural center.'"[141] China contained one-fourth of the world's population, which together with its burgeoning economy and the switch to silver, spelled well-nigh insatiable demand. It was not until the mid-17th century that the gold/silver ratio in China rose to a level comparable with Europe. Up until that point, not only silks and porcelain but gold were funneled to the European economy, and silver was funneled out.

Much of the silver absorbed by China came from Spanish America, through the direct Acapulco-to-Manila trade route; in fact, Flynn and Giráldez date the establishment of a truly global economy, connecting all the great continents in one system, from the founding of Manila in 1571.[142] But then again, a great deal was also shipped from Europe to the East by

---

Monetary Crisis," *The Journal of Economic History*, Vol. 56, No. 2, Papers Presented at the Fifty-Fifth Annual Meeting of the Economic History Association (Jun., 1996), p. 430.

[139]Harriet T. Zurndorfer, "Another Look at China, Money, Silver, and the Seventeenth-Century Crisis," *Journal of the Economic and Social History of the Orient*, Vol. 42, No. 3 (1999), p. 403.

[140]Dennis O. Flynn and Arturo Giráldez, "Born with a 'Silver Spoon': The Origin of World Trade in 1571," *Journal of World History*, vol. 6, no. 2 (Fall, 1995), p. 206.

[141]Von Glahn, "Myth and Reality of China's Seventeenth-Century Monetary Crisis," p. 433.

[142]Flynn and Giráldez, "Born with a 'Silver Spoon,'" p. 201.

the newly founded East India Companies of Holland and England, while the more familiar Mediterranean-Levantine route continued in service as well.[143]

For a long while there was enough silver to go around for everyone, especially for Spain, which used the profits from its silver trade to maintain multi-front wars and generally act as the moralizing bully of Europe. The astounding ramifications of this have yet to be realized by scholars of early-modern European history. "The silver-industry profits that financed the Spanish empire were huge because China had become the world's dominant silver customer. This implies that ultimately China was responsible for a power shift within early modern Europe. In the absence of the 'silverization' of China, it is hard to imagine how Castile could have financed simultaneous wars for generations against the Ottomans in the Mediterranean; Protestant England and Holland and the French in Europe, the New World, and Asia; and against indigenous peoples in the Philippines."[144] China financed the Catholic Counter-reformation!

But there is an even greater ramification than this. For the "silverization" of China also helped to finance the return of gold to the position of primacy in the European monetary system. The enormous profits generated by the silver trade led to the scouring of European countries for silver and the export of it whenever the mint rates made it profitable to do so. This was especially the case in England, where the East India Company engendered bad blood by pursuing a policy of silver export in the face of a scarcity of coin for domestic use.

Feavearyear provides the dreary details of the shift in England. "A few figures will perhaps serve to illustrate the completeness of the change-over from silver to gold. From the accession of Queen Elizabeth in 1558 to the foundation of the Bank of England in 1694 the total amount of gold coined at the Mint did not amount upon a liberal estimate to 15 millions, and nearly a half of this was in guineas coined after 1663. From 1695, however, until 1740 the amount of gold turned out was over 17 millions. On the other hand, while in the former period the amount of silver coined

---

[143]The latter serviced the Muslim countries and India, but even then, the eventual destination was always China.

[144]Flynn and Giráldez, "Born with a 'Silver Spoon,'" pp. 210-211.

was over 20 millions (much of it, it must be admitted, forced artificially into the Mint), during the latter period the quantity dealt with, after the recoinage was completed, even if we include £320,000 issued in 1707 in a recoinage

Figure 16. English five-guinea piece, minted during the reign of Charles II. Source: Classical Numismatic Group, Inc. http://www.cngcoins.com.

at Edinburgh, amounted to barely a million."[145] The East India Company was, of course, a major beneficiary of this policy. For example: "An absurd attempt was made in 1708 to encourage the minting of silver by setting aside £6,000 to pay a premium of 2 ½ d. an ounce upon silver brought to the Mint. This amounted to nothing less than a bonus to the East India Company, and when the money was exhausted the metal ceased to come." Feavearyear's summary is conclusive:

> For all practical purposes the Mint was closed to the coinage of silver during the greater part of the eighteenth century. The market price was never less than 1 ½ d. an ounce above the Mint price. In thirty-seven out of the hundred years no silver was coined at all; in ten others the amount was less than £1,000; and the total for the whole of the century was only £1,254,000. It seems clear that a great proportion of the heavy silver coins issued by William III had disappeared before the death of Queen Anne, while on the other hand so persistent was the influx of gold that most of the heavy issues of that metal must have been added to the circulation or to the reserves of the bankers.[146]

The silver shortage hit hardest at the level of the common citizen, precisely as it had during the previous "silver famine" in the late Middle Ages. "The silver coinage was by now in a lamentable condition .... so long

---

[145]Albert Feavearyear, *The Pound Sterling: A History of English Money*, 2nd ed. (Oxford: Clarendon Press, 1963), p. 158.

[146]Feavearyear, *The Pound Sterling*, p. 158.

as the Government was unable to find a method of providing the country
with a sound and adequate coinage, the importation and issue of counterfeit
or light silver was a good thing .... The counterfeiter tended to fill up the
void" left by the Mint's neglect.[147] "A printed ballad of 1721 which asked 'O
Yes! O Yes! Can any say / Where all the Money's run away', echoed a popular lament about the effect of poor coinage on trade, and by 1750 things
had deteriorated to the extent that one writer was able to remark that 'Of
counterfeit Half-pence there are now almost infinite Sorts.'"[148]

Now counterfeiting was not a risk-free proposition. Considered
treason under English law – coinage being a prerogative of the sovereign –
the punishment was set, for men, at drawing and quartering, and, for
women, at burning at the stake.[149] But in the English system, of course, the
accused was tried by a jury, and juries were composed of the same people
so inconvenienced by the lack of a functioning medium of exchange. Along
with difficulties in gathering evidence, getting witnesses, and the like, this
made it difficult to obtain convictions.[150] For counterfeiting was an activity
for which "the line between legality and illegality was blurred."[151] It is pa-
thetic testimony to the recalcitrance of the English monetary authorities to
act in a responsible manner – but then again, all of this becomes understandable when one realizes that monetary authorities were acting not in the
nation's interest, but the bankers'.

---

[147]Feavearyear, *The Pound Sterling*, p. 169.
[148]Malcolm Gaskill, *Crime and Mentalities in Early Modern England* (Cambridge,
England: Cambridge University Press, 2000), p. 164.
[149]Gaskill, *Crime and Mentalities in Early Modern England*, p. 127.
[150]Gaskill, *Crime and Mentalities in Early Modern England*, pp. 152ff.
[151]Gaskill, *Crime and Mentalities in Early Modern England*, p. 164.

11. NATURAL LIBERTY AND
CLASSICAL ECONOMICS

The English authorities' attitude of wilful indifference in the face of currency shortage was more than mere recalcitrance. The mindset of the age was shifting away from the mercantilism of the age of coinage, toward the philosophy of classical economics, with its emphasis on market forces. The new system of money, based as it was on commodities, was one that depended upon those forces. Therefore, money shortages were simply viewed as market phenomena, beyond the reach of monetary authorities even if they should desire to intervene. And intervention itself was now called into question too.

The new theory provided the ideology to pass judgment on the people whose lives were rendered desperate by the lack of a functioning medium of exchange. "The doctrine that we have been inculcating is so contrary to the common notions, that a want of money is a common cry," wrote one of the new apologists, William Harris, in 1757 – at the height of the scarcity of coin. "All the scramble is for money; few think they have enough, and many complain. This probably will be ever the case, nor would setting the mint to work cure the evil; and perhaps there is no where more want, than where there is most money."[152]

For according to the new economic doctrine, the fault lay not with the lack of provision of a functioning money supply but with those people whose lives were rendered economically unworkable. "The complaints of particular persons arise, not from a deficiency of money or counters in circulation; but from their own want of property, want of skill, address, or opportunity of getting more money; or perhaps only for want of frugality, in spending more than their income or proper share."[153] So easy to write

---

[152]William Harris, *An Essay Upon Money and Coins, Part I, the Theories of Commerce, Money, and Exchanges* (London: G. Hawkins, 1757), pp. 103-104.

[153]Harris, *An Essay Upon Money and Coins*, pp. 104-105.

from behind the desk! And the provision of a more ample money supply
would do nothing to cure the ills of the complainants; for it is their own
lack of industry or want of customers that is the root of the problem.
Therefore Mr. Harris offers this well-meaning advice:

> A greater plenty of money would not mend or better their
> condition; those who have it, will not be persuaded to purchase
> more of this or that commodity, than what their own wants,
> conveniency, or fancy prompt them to; and those who cannot make
> so much profit in their respective professions as formerly, must
> either turn themselves some other way, or be content to live more
> frugally. But all will not be wise in time; emulation in show is a pow-
> erful incentive; few can bear the thoughts of retrenching while it is
> yet time, and many finding themselves upon the decline, will grow
> desperate and precipitate themselves the faster. In all great towns,
> bankruptcies will happen, and perhaps no where more frequent,
> than where wealth and money most abound. These evils, if upon the
> whole they be evils, are what the mines cannot cure, but are rather
> what have been introduced and fostered by them.[154]

These evils were introduced by the mines? Hard currency is the
problem then? If Harris really meant this, perhaps he could have offered an
alternative, instead of a perfunctory "deal with it." Harris thought he was
cleverly dismissing the mercantilist "preoccupation" with metal. In fact, this
was the beginning of an unholy alliance between doctrinaire theory, purporting to be the epitome of natural justice, and nefarious, class-oriented
practice. For the new monetary system fostered the primacy of one class
above all others – the "capitalist," i.e., specie-possessing class. In the following century, the unfortunate consequences of this approach would
prompt the reaction of the labor movement, socialism, and communism.
Free-market theory had allowed itself to become the champion of this
bullion-based system, so that it could gain primacy over its antagonist, mercantilism. The result would be a fatal association with that system and the
discrimination and oppression inherent to it.

---

[154]Harris, *An Essay Upon Money and Coins*, pp. 105-106.

A new age had dawned. The Enlightenment brought with it new-found understanding regarding law and the state. Mercantilism gave way to Natural Law and Natural Rights. And according to the new school, all that was needed to promote the Wealth of Nations – the title of one of the key texts to come out of this period, indicating the change in priorities from the mercantilist conflict of interests to a natural harmony of interests among the nations[155] – is for market forces to be left unrestrained. This would result in a harmony of interests and an equilibrium of supply and demand, of pro-ducer and consumer, of nation and nation. Adam Smith's "invisible hand" would lead otherwise self-centered individuals to promote the common good, even if unbeknownst to themselves.[156]

Because there is a great deal of truth in Smith's reasoning, it is all the more important properly to understand the flaw in it. And that flaw is this: there are no market forces operating in a state of nature, in the way that Smith and the other proponents of the Natural Law school of economics viewed it. Economies function within the parameters set by particular soci-eties, comprising a range of institutions that condition and act upon those market forces. These institutions are not just there; they rise and fall, they change over time, they become better and become worse. They condition market forces, and they must be accounted for by market forces. Market forces do not operate within an institutional vacuum, and the use of the word "nature" is a fig leaf obscuring this reality.

---

[155]Adam Smith, *An Inquiry Into the Nature and Causes of the Wealth of Nations,* originally published in 1776, and available in many editions thereafter.

[156]"As every individual, therefore, endeavours as much as he can both to employ his capital in the support of domestic industry, and so to direct that indus-try that its produce may be of the greatest value; every individual necessarily labours to render the annual revenue of the society as great as he can. He generally, indeed, neither intends to promote the public interest, nor knows how much he is promot-ing it. By preferring the support of domestic to that of foreign industry, he intends only his own security; and by directing that industry in such a manner as its pro-duce may be of the greatest value, he intends only his own gain, and he is in this, as in many other cases, led by an invisible hand to promote an end which was no part of his intention. Nor is it always the worse for the society that it was no part of it. By pursuing his own interest he frequently promotes that of the society more effectually than when he really intends to promote it." Smith, *The Wealth of Nations,* Book 4, Chapter 2.

Chief among these institutions are the legal system (or lack thereof) and, closely connected with this, the monetary system. The Smithian system assumes a pre-legal situation in which "truck, barter, and exchange" between individuals simply happens, the result of a "certain propensity in human nature;" supposedly, our modern economic system is the direct descendant of this state of affairs.[157] But there is much more to the evolution of economic systems than that.[158]

The argument to this point has repeatedly shown the importance of the monetary system to the economy at large. But the natural-law economists (who have since become known as the classical economists), reacting against the received mercantilist emphasis on metallic currency, threw out the baby with the bath water. Against the one-sided emphasis on the retention of precious metal within the economy, they swung, as if on a pendulum, completely to the other side of the argument, stating categorically that the currency was irrelevant to wealth creation, that in fact wealth consisted not in money but in the goods and services produced and ultimately consumed, and that when money was treated as wealth, it only served to hide this ultimate truth. Economists call this "the veil of money," and consider it their duty to remove that veil so as to discover the "true" or "natural" economy.

But money – the kind of it, the quality of it, the manipulation of it – is not so easily dismissed. Granted, classical economics understood this enough to be able to argue that money could pose a problem. What was needed was simply to leave the market to determine what kind of money should be used. Over time, the precious metals had been chosen; they were the "most marketable commodity," as the phrase goes. The use of commodity money was thus the solution to all monetary problems.

In this manner, classical economics – the bastion of freedom-loving patriots, intensely suspicious of the activities both of the state and of private bankers (who would come to be known as the Money Power) argued just

---

[157]Smith, *The Wealth of Nations*, Book 1, Chapter 2.
[158]This is developed in detail in Alvarado, *Common Law & Natural Rights*, chs. 5 and 6; *Investing in the New Normal: Beyond the Keynesian Endpoint* (Aalten: WordBridge Publishing, 2010), ch. 1.

the case that the Money Power wished to have argued. It ensured the hammerlock of the merchant bankers over the economies of the nations for more than a century.

12. THE AUTOMATIC MECHANISM

The logic of natural liberty was used to justify the shift to gold in the English economy in the 18th century. One of the gold standard's leading proponents, William Shaw, put the matter bluntly. "The verdict of history on the great problem of the nineteenth century – bimetallism – is clear and crushing and final, and against the evidence of history no gainsaying of theory ought for a moment to stand."[159]

Bimetallism was the 19th century's version of state-controlled coinage, entailing a state-decreed exchange rate for gold versus silver. In celebrating the "crushing" defeat of bimetallism and the triumph of gold, Shaw saw only the victory of "natural" market forces over state control of currency. "The ceasing of the artificial arbitrary Mint rates made way for a naturally determined or *commercial* ratio, and the regulation of the international flow of the precious metals was left to the oscillation of trade balances, and to the action of interest rates and discount. The change is one from a mediaeval, State-bound, merely legislative system to the modern system, in which the flow of precious metals is determined by the perfectly natural and automatic action of international trade."[160]

The currency systems of the nations of the world had switched over to the "perfectly natural and automatic" determinations of market forces. Shaw likens the operation of these market forces to machinery – a useful analogy when one wishes to attribute a technocratic disinterestedness to one's policy preferences. This is how it worked:

---

[159]William A. Shaw, *The History of Currency 1252 to 1894* (London: Wilsons & Milne, 1896), pp. vii-viii. The verdict against bimetallism is anything but crushing. See Irving Fisher, "The Mechanics of Bimetallism," in *The Economic Journal*, Vol. 4, No. 15 (Sep., 1894), pp. 527-537; Milton Friedman, "Bimetallism Revisited," in *The Journal of Economic Perspectives*, Vol. 4, No. 4 (Autumn, 1990), pp. 85-104; and above all, Marc Flandreau, *The Glitter of Gold: France, Bimetallism, and the Emergence of the International Gold Standard, 1848-1873*, trans. Owen Leeming (Oxford, England: Oxford University Press, 2004).

[160]Shaw, *The History of Currency*, pp. 160-161.

Between a circle of commercially interconnected countries, and over a certain cycle of time or operations, there is an equivalence of exchange of goods and services. Movements of currency in the most elementary form assist the process, as far as immediate settlements are concerned; bills of exchange assist it when there is need of deferred payments … and, finally, bank and discount rates assist the process by providing currency media at times and places which would otherwise be unable to attract a supply.… The machinery by which that equilibrium is accomplished is currency in the widest sense. The index or indicator and safety-valve of the whole is the rate of interest. On these bank rates are based the operations of the modern bullion dealers or arbitragists, which serve to equalise or economise the distribution of the precious metals all over the world.[161]

So there are "bills of exchange," "bank and discount rates," the "rate of interest" which acts as "indicator and safety-valve of the whole." And are there actual persons behind all of this? Yes, there are: the "modern bullion dealers and arbitragists." But what is the difference between these "modern" market makers and the ones prior to the advent of this mechanism? After all, Shaw does not cast their activities in a favorable light. "The monetary system of Europe," he writes on page 72, "unconsciously bimetallic and with an appalling variety of ratio prevalent at the same moment in different places – lay open, helpless and defenceless, and inviting to the bullionist, financier, or arbitragist." And on page 165 he writes, "In the seventeenth century there was no conception of theory at all, and the practical difficulty was how to frustrate the operations of the bullionist and arbitragist and politicians, and the depletion of national treasure due to their activity, and based on a difference of ratio prevailing in different countries." But now the nations were to acquiesce in a system whereby these activities are put in the light of a disinterested machinery? Could it not have been that it was precisely the goal of the "bullionist, financier, or arbitragist" to implement a "machinery" putting himself in control of the currency, not of one nation, but of all the nations at once?

---

[161]Shaw, *The History of Currency*, pp. 165-166.

Indeed, this constituted a triumph of prodigious proportions. Over time, this banking hegemony was achieved by laboriously overthrowing the state-managed system of coinage to establish a commodity-money system whereby the "most marketable commodity," as it is termed – but can better be termed the "most market-cornerable commodity"[162] – was established as legal tender. This was achieved in England in surreptitious manner, through the systematic ensconcement of gold as the country's currency, and the concurrent *de facto* abandonment of silver.

The vehicle by which the gold currency triumphed was the Bank of England, which received a monopoly on the issue of bank notes, and which was allowed to issue notes far in excess of "cash" reserves – cash, at this time, meaning gold, whether in coins or bullion. By this means, a state-sponsored monopoly reserve bank was put in charge of the nation's money. And in true English fashion, there was never any legislation or declaration of such intent; one thing led to another, and before anyone knew it, the Bank of England was the custodian of the nation's monetized wealth.[163]

In banking parlance, the Bank of England became the lender of last resort. Although the Bank was dragged into this role kicking and screaming, it was a role that developed in the nature of the case, given England's "decision" to establish a gold standard for its currency. By making this scarce, costly commodity the sole final store of value and medium of exchange in its economy, England delivered itself over to the power of those banks – and the individuals behind them – who controlled that commodity. This ultimate power over the money base gave bankers a mechanism of control absolutely astounding in its scope and implications.

---

[162]One 19th-century pamphlet emphasized just this aspect: F.W. Bain, *The Corner in Gold* (London: James Parker and Co., 1893).

[163]"With so many advantages over all competitors, it is quite natural that the Bank of England should have far outstripped them all. Inevitably it became *the* bank in London; all the other bankers grouped themselves round it, and lodged their reserve with it. Thus our *one*-reserve system of banking was not deliberately founded upon definite reasons; it was the gradual consequence of many singular events, and of an accumulation of legal privileges on a single bank which has now been altered, and which no one would now defend." Walter Bagehot, *Lombard Street: A Description of the Money Market* (New York: Charles Scribner's Sons, 1897 [1873]), pp. 99-100.

Behind this mechanism were structural advantages beyond the legislation-decreed preeminence enjoyed by the Bank. One of these was the direct role it played in financing government budgets. In exchange for its loans, it received securities against which it could issue bank notes, which, because convertible into gold, enjoyed the status of gold. Secondly, it was intimately connected with the East India Company from the time of its origin, when the government of William III was strapped for cash.[164] It was therefore a primary recipient of the gold the East India Company brought in from the East, which it used to bolster its reserves. By these means and others, the Bank of England came to be the custodian of the lion's share of the nation's currency.

Other banks developed the practice of storing reserves with the Bank, which solidified its central-bank status. As Walter Bagehot explained, "the same reasons which make it desirable for a private person to keep a banker make it also desirable for every banker, as respects his reserve, to bank with another banker if he safely can. The custody of very large sums in solid cash entails much care, and some cost; everyone wishes to shift these upon others if he can do so without suffering. Accordingly, the other bankers of London, having perfect confidence in the Bank of England, get that bank to keep their reserve for them."[165] And the country banks spread across the rest of England likewise kept accounts with the Bank, leading to the situation where the entire country's banking reserves were lodged with one institution. That institution, in turn, took those reserves and lent above and beyond them. Actual bank reserves hereby came to be a fraction of nominal currency outstanding.

---

[164]"Twice William Paterson submitted a proposal which was to provide the King with the necessary funds, whilst those who advanced the money were to be considered as founders of a National Bank. Each time his efforts were in vain. In 1694 Michael Godfrey and some others who experienced financial difficulties in connection with the East India Company, invoked Paterson's aid. A third project was devised on the same lines as the two former ones. In consideration of an annual payment of £100,000 the promoters undertook to find a capital of £1,200,000 on behalf of the Government. Thanks to their influence, this scheme was successful." W. R. Bisschop, *The Rise of the London Money Market 1640-1826* (London: P.S. King and Son, 1910), pp. 68-69.

[165]Bagehot, *Lombard Street*, p. 27.

With the publication of his groundbreaking book *Lombard Street* in 1873, Bagehot ("I am by no means an alarmist"[166]) sounded the alarm. "The main effect is to cause the reserve to be much smaller in proportion to the liabilities than it would otherwise be. The reserve of the London bankers being on deposit in the Bank of England, the Bank always lends a principal part of it…. We see then that the banking reserve of the Bank of England – some 10,000,000 *l.* on an average of years now, and formerly much less – is all which is held against the liabilities of Lombard Street; and if that were all, we might well be amazed at the immense development of our credit system." But that is not all, for the country bankers do this too, as do Scotch and Irish bankers. "All their spare money is in London, and is invested as all other London money now is; and, therefore, the reserve in the Banking Department of the Bank of England is the banking reserve not only of the Bank of England, but of all London – and not only of all London, but of all England, Ireland, and Scotland too."[167]

Although already an obviously precarious situation, it gets worse. For by this time, London had become the reserve bank not only for England, Ireland, and Scotland, but also for foreign countries such as Germany, likewise parking their gold reserves with the Bank of England.

> Of late there has been a still further increase in our liabilities. Since the Franco-German war, we may be said to keep the European reserve also. Deposit Banking is indeed so small on the Continent, that no large reserve need be held on account of it. A reserve of the same sort which is needed in England and Scotland is not needed abroad. But all great communities have at times to pay large sums in cash, and of that cash a great store must be kept somewhere. Formerly there were two such stores in Europe, one was the Bank of France, and the other the Bank of England. But since the suspension of specie payments by the Bank of France, its use as a reservoir of specie is at an end. No one can draw a cheque on it and be sure of getting gold or silver for that cheque. Accordingly the

---

[166]Bagehot, *Lombard Street*, p. 20.
[167]Bagehot, *Lombard Street*, pp. 29-31.

whole liability for such international payments in cash is thrown on the Bank of England.[168]

These foreign-owned reserves were crucial. The vicissitudes of the balance of payments could lead to their withdrawal at a moment's notice, triggering the dreaded "run on the bank" for which reserves were entirely insufficient. "Now that London is the clearing-house to foreign countries, London has a new liability to foreign countries. At whatever place many people have to make payments, at that place those people must keep money. A large deposit of foreign money in London is now necessary for the business of the world."[169]

This exposed not only the Bank of England but the entire domestic economy to foreign influence. The "automatic mechanism" of the international gold standard requires balances of payments between countries to be equalized by gold transfers. As international commerce increases, the reserves drawn upon to restore imbalances must also increase. And with a large amount of those reserves actually held by foreigners, the health of the banking system hangs in the foreign-sentiment balance. "The deposit at a clearing-house necessary to settle the balance of commerce must tend to increase as that commerce itself increases. And this foreign deposit is evidently of a delicate and peculiar nature. It depends on the good opinion of foreigners, and that opinion may diminish or may change into a bad opinion.... And we may reasonably presume that in proportion as we augment the deposits of cash by foreigners in London, we augment both the chances and the disasters of a 'run' upon England. And if that run should happen, the bullion to meet it must be taken from the Bank. There is no other large store in the country."[170]

So here we have a better view of Shaw's "perfectly natural and automatic" machinery. Indeed, Bagehot agrees with Shaw that the system functions in terms of market forces – "The value of money is settled, like that of all other commodities, by supply and demand, and only the form is essen-

[168]Bagehot, pp. 31-32.
[169]Bagehot, p. 33.
[170]Bagehot, p. 34.

tially different."[171] And Bagehot agrees with Shaw that interest rates are the means to raise and lower the value of money, the means by which that mechanism balancing international payments functions. "If the interest of money be raised, it is proved by experience that money *does* come to Lombard Street, and theory shows that it *ought* to come.... Continental bankers and others instantly send great sums here, as soon as the rate of interest shows that it can be done profitably.... And there is also a slower mercantile operation. The rise in the rate of discount acts immediately on the trade of this country." Furthermore, "whatever persons – one bank or many banks – in any country hold the banking reserve of that country, ought at the very beginning of an unfavourable foreign exchange at once to raise the rate of interest, so as to prevent their reserve from being diminished farther, and so as to replenish it by imports of bullion."[172]

This logic was used by John Stuart Mill to argue that gold supplies could be supplemented simply by adhering to the same rules as other commodities. Answering criticism of his position, he asked, "What hinders gold, or any other commodity whatever, from being 'increased as fast as all other valuable things put together?' If the produce of the world, in all commodities taken together, should come to be doubled, what is to prevent the annual produce of gold from being doubled likewise? ... Unless it can be proved that the production of bullion cannot be increased by the application of increased labour and capital, it is evident that the stimulus of an increased value of the commodity will have the same effect in extending the mining operations, as it is admitted to have in all other branches of production."[173] But such increases in bullion production are precisely what cannot be proved. This is the limiting factor that ensures an upward trend in the value of gold.

Anticipating this objection, Mill goes on: "But, secondly, even if the currency could not be increased at all, and if every addition to the aggregate

---

[171]Bagehot, p. 113.

[172]Bagehot, pp. 45-46.

[173]John Stuart Mill, *Principles of Political Economy with some of their Applications to Social Philosophy,* William J. Ashley, ed. (London; Longmans, Green and Co., 1909), III.13.12, n. 43.

produce of the country must necessarily be accompanied by a proportional diminution of general prices; it is incomprehensible how any person who has attended to the subject can fail to see that a fall of price, thus produced, is no loss to producers: they receive less money; but the smaller amount goes exactly as far, in all expenditure, whether productive or personal, as the larger quantity did before. The only difference would be in the increased burthen of fixed money payments; and of that (coming, as it would, very gradually) a very small portion would fall on the productive classes, who have rarely any debts of old standing, and who would suffer almost solely in the increased onerousness of their contribution to the taxes which pay the interest of the National Debt." Such explaining-away of the effects of deflation is sheer wishful thinking, and reality repeatedly proved this statement wrong.[174] But the sentiment lived on at the Bank of England: "the traditional rule of the bank stated that a 10 percent bank rate would draw gold out of the ground itself."[175]

What are the implications of such a position? Interest rates are raised and lowered simply because other countries have more or less demand for gold. In other words, the entire domestic economy rises and falls, is stimulated or depressed, by the vagaries of the international gold market, and hence of economic and financial conditions in any foreign country or countries which may or may not, for whatever reason, desire gold or dump it. Thus, during the downturn of the 1870s, "while the German Government was collecting gold for one reason, the French for a second, the American was collecting it for a third. There was little left to come to England. It was impossible to cure the slump – not because there was not the productive capacity to produce more goods, but because there was not sufficient gold at the apex of the inverted pyramid of credit to finance the increased productivity.... What a system – a system that punished with atrophy the whole productive life of England because of other policies that were no

---

[174]Mill, *Principles of Political Economy*, III.13.12, n. 43. Perhaps this is why this section, first included in the second edition of 1849, was removed in the 5th edition of 1862. See the Library of Economics and Liberty [Online] version, available at http://www.econlib.org/library/Mill/mlP42.html.

[175]Quigley, *Tragedy and Hope*, p. 347.

more connected with that life than were the activities of the man in the moon!"[176]

One commodity market, and a "thin" one at that, held the fate of national economies in its hands. "Periods of internal panic and external demand for bullion commonly occur together.... We must look first to the foreign drain, and raise the rate of interest as high as may be necessary. Unless you can stop the foreign export, you cannot allay the domestic alarm."[177]

It was Samuel Loyd, Lord Overstone – "perhaps, the greatest financier of modern times"[178] – who was the architect of this mechanism. Loyd was behind the Bank Act of 1844, by which the currency of England was rigidly restricted to a gold-specie money base – who, in Adams' words, by this means "succeeded in laying his grasp upon the currency of the kingdom."[179]

Loyd comprehended this bullion-based system's permanent potential of enriching the creditor at the expense of the debtor, benefitting the possessors of wealth at the expense of those who produce it. "Certainly he understood as few men, even of later generations, have understood, the mighty engine of the single standard. He comprehended that, with expanding trade, an inelastic currency must rise in value; he saw that, with sufficient resources at command, his class might be able to establish such a rise, almost at pleasure; certainly that they could manipulate it when it came, by taking advantage of foreign exchanges." The mechanism of foreign exchange thus could be leveraged to the advantage of the creditor: "a contraction of the currency might be forced to an extreme, and that when money rose beyond price, as in 1825, debtors would have to surrender their property on such terms as creditors might dictate," which property might then be resold at a profit when gold resumed its influx and prices again began

---

[176]Hollis, *The Two Nations*, p. 173.

[177]Bagehot, p. 56.

[178]"Cautious and sagacious, though resolute and bold, gifted with an amazing penetration into the complex causes which control the competition of modern life, he swayed successive administrations, and crushed down the fiercest opposition." Adams, *The Law of Civilization and Decay*, p. 335.

[179]Adams, *Law of Civilization and Decay*, p. 336.

rising.[180] Hence, a mechanism for expropriating wealth from the middle class and depositing it in the hands of wealthy capitalists. Given such a system, it is no wonder that anti-capitalism took hold.

In practice, Loyd's engine functioned just as he smugly envisioned it. As he testified to a Parliamentary committee in 1847, "Monetary distress tends to produce fall of prices; that fall of prices encourages exports and diminishes imports; consequently it tends to promote an influx of bullion;" therefore, falling prices are a natural phenomenon and a necessary prerequisite for a return to growth. "As followed out by his successors, Loyd's policy has not only forced down prices throughout the West, but has changed the aspect of civilization. In England the catastrophe began with the passage of the Bank Act," of 1845, the work of Prime Minister Robert Peel, Loyd's "lieutenant."[181]

The upshot of this situation was a system centered on the Bank of England but extending across the Western world, whereby international bankers controlled national economies. "The merchant bankers of London had already at hand in 1810-1850 the Stock Exchange, the Bank of England, and the London money market.... In time they brought into their financial network the provincial banking centers, organized as commercial banks and savings banks, as well as insurance companies, to form all of these into a single financial system on an international scale which manipulated the quantity and flow of money so that they were able to influence, if not control, governments on one side and industries on the other."[182]

This control rested on the acceptance, by governments and industry, of two basic "axioms," as Quigley terms them, both of which "were based on the assumption that politicians were too weak and too subject to temporary popular pressures to be trusted with control of the money system." According to these axioms, "the sanctity of all values and the soundness of money must be protected in two ways: by basing the value of money on gold and by allowing bankers to control the supply of money. To do this it

---

[180]Adams, *Law of Civilization and Decay*, p. 337-338.
[181]Adams, *Law of Civilization and Decay*, pp. 336, 338, 339.
[182]Quigley, *Tragedy and Hope*, p. 51.

was necessary to conceal, or even to mislead, both governments and people about the nature of money and its methods of operation."[183]

The shibboleth of "stabilization" was just such an example of bankers' deception, claiming as it did that it was necessary for them to manage the currency, established on gold, to attain the stabilization of prices and foreign exchange. But as Quigley notes, this "really achieved only stabilization of exchanges, while its influence on prices were quite independent and incidental, and might be unstabilizing (from its usual tendency to force prices downward by limiting the supply of money)." Such a program of stabilization actually destabilized prices domestically.[184]

In fact, the 19th century witnessed repeated bouts of whipsaw boom-and-bust generated precisely by this so-called "automatic mechanism" of "stabilization." Prime Minister Robert Peel "spoke of having put the country back upon an 'automatic metallic currency' and of a return to 'the ancient right standard of England.'"[185] But there was nothing of ancient right about it, and the automatic machinery actually ceased functioning whenever put under sufficient strain. It was the principle of the money multiplier, a function of fractional-reserve banking, that guaranteed its own failure, as practice sufficiently demonstrated.[186] By this "automatic" mechanism, then, every time one pound of gold should leave the country, 10 pounds in paper money or other currency would have to be withdrawn from circulation. Hence, the smallest shifts in foreign exchange had a multiplier effect on domestic prices. Furthermore, in the case of a supplementation to the gold stock, the inflationary effect might materialize or it might not, depending on

---

[183]Quigley, *Tragedy and Hope*, p. 53.

[184]Quigley, *Tragedy and Hope*, p. 53.

[185]Christopher Hollis, *The Two Nations: A Financial Study of English History* (London: G. Routledge and Sons, 1935), p. 97.

[186]"It is not necessary to follow through the monotonous and dreary story of the breakdown of Peel's system every single time that it was subjected to any strain from 1821 to 1931.... The amount of money in circulation, under Peel's system, obviously depends upon the amount of gold in the country. If the banks as a rule lend ten Promises to Pay for every pound of gold that they possess – the proportion which they soon adopted – then if £1 of gold leaves the country, £10 of Promises to Pay have to be withdrawn from circulation by the banks refusing to make new loans when old loans have been repaid." Hollis, *The Two Nations*, p. 98.

the course of lending; but in the case of a diminution, the deflationary effect must materialize *of necessity*. "If an ounce of gold was added to the point of the pyramid in a system where law and custom allowed 10 percent reserves on each level, it *could permit* an increase of deposits equivalent to $2067 on the uppermost level. If such an ounce of gold were withdrawn from a fully expanded pyramid of money, this *would compel* a reduction of deposits by at least this amount, probably by a refusal to renew loans."[187]

Quigley's ruminations on the power of these bankers are telling. "On the whole," he writes in his seminal work *Tragedy and Hope*, "in the period up to 1931, bankers, especially the Money Power controlled by the international investment bankers, were able to dominate both business and government. They could dominate business, especially in activities and in areas where industry could not finance its own needs for capital, because investment bankers had the ability to supply or refuse to supply such capital."[188] And as far as governments were concerned, the need for credit was one obvious such tool, but "bankers could steer governments in ways they wished them to go by other pressures" as well. "Since most government officials felt ignorant of finance, they sought advice from bankers whom they considered to be experts in the field." Which led them to do things they otherwise wouldn't, given the consequences. "The history of the last century shows … that the advice given to governments by bankers, like the advice they gave to industrialists, was consistently good for bankers, but was often disastrous for governments, businessmen, and the people generally." Governments might not immediately accede to such good advice; in that case, it "could be enforced if necessary by manipulation of exchanges, gold flows, discount rates, and even levels of business activity. Thus Morgan dominated Cleveland's second administration by gold withdrawals, and in 1936-1938 French foreign exchange manipulators paralyzed the Popular Front governments."[189]

McNair Wilson draws a similar picture. "By acquiring the power to export gold … its owners acquired the right to change the level of price of

---

[187]Quigley, *Tragedy and Hope*, p. 57.
[188]Quigley, *Tragedy and Hope*, p. 60.
[189]Quigley, *Tragedy and Hope*, p. 62.

goods both in the country from which the gold was taken and in the country into which they chose to send it.... The Money power has acquired the right of creating demand and also of abolishing it at its pleasure, and so, in effect, has set itself in the place of humanity as well as in the place of Kings. When it wills that production shall take place it expands credit; when it wills that production shall cease, credit is restricted. Thus boom and slump may be made to follow each other in endless succession."[190]

Hollis's conclusion is succinct: "[The gold standard's] virtue was not that it gave the country a stable monetary system but, on the contrary, that it put it within the power of a few determined men to plunge the country into chaos whenever they wanted to."[191]

---

[190]McNair Wilson, *Monarchy or Money Power?*, ch. XV.
[191]Hollis, *The Two Nations,* p. 106.

13. THE SOCIAL QUESTION
UNRAVELED

In a well-known passage, John Maynard Keynes provided a lucid picture of the pre-1914 era:

> The inhabitant of London could order by telephone, sipping his morning tea in bed, the various products of the whole earth, in such quantity as he might see fit, and reasonably expect their early delivery upon his doorstep; he could at the same moment and by the same means adventure his wealth in the natural resources and new enterprises of any quarter of the world, and share, without exertion or even trouble, in their prospective fruits and advantages; or he could decide to couple the security of his fortunes with the good faith of the townspeople of any substantial municipality in any continent that fancy or information might recommend. He could secure forthwith, if he wished it, cheap and comfortable means of transit to any country or climate without passport or other formality, could despatch his servant to the neighboring office of a bank for such supply of the precious metals as might seem convenient, and could then proceed abroad to foreign quarters, without knowledge of their religion, language, or customs, bearing coined wealth upon his person, and would consider himself greatly aggrieved and much surprised at the least interference. But, most important of all, he regarded this state of affairs as normal, certain, and permanent, except in the direction of further improvement, and any deviation from it as aberrant, scandalous, and avoidable. The projects and politics of militarism and imperialism, of racial and cultural rivalries, of monopolies, restrictions, and exclusion, which were to play the serpent to this paradise, were little more than the amusements of his daily newspaper, and appeared to exercise almost no influence at all on

the ordinary course of social and economic life, the internationaliza-
tion of which was nearly complete in practice.[192]

This easy internationalism was by no means the whole story.[193] Free
trade was indeed the corollary to the gold standard, otherwise the entire
system would fall flat. But free trade, combined with fixed exchange rates –
fixed because all currencies were tied to gold – meant that gold outflows
could only be compensated by falling prices, which then would cause the
trade deficit to swing to surplus, thus bringing gold back into the country.
Behold the automatic mechanism, so highly thought of – in Quigley's view,
"one of the greatest social instruments ever devised by man."[194] It is astounding to realize that such a system, embodying as it did such massive
swings in domestic price levels, could ever have been accepted as norma-
tive.

The U.S. Senate *Report of the Monetary Commission* of 1876 had earlier
elucidated the devastating effect falling prices have on the economy. The
report was presented three years into a debilitating recession in the wake of
the U.S. demonetizing silver in 1873. "The great and still continuing fall in
prices in the United States has proved most disastrous to nearly every industrial enterprise," said the *Report*. "The bitter experience of the last few
years has been an expensive but most thorough teacher. It has taught capitalists neither to invest in nor loan money on such enterprises, and just as
thoroughly has it taught business men not to borrow for the purpose of
inaugurating or prosecuting them."[195] Businessmen, entrepreneurs, stock-
holders, indeed all forms of capital put out for profitable ventures, suffered

---

[192]John Maynard Keynes, *The Economic Consequences of the Peace* (New York:
Harcourt, Brace, and Howe, Inc., 1920), II.4.
[193]Keynes indeed paints a glowing picture even of the situation of the working classes: "The greater part of the population, it is true, worked hard and lived at
a low standard of comfort, yet were, to all appearances, reasonably contented with
this lot" (Keynes, *Economic Consequences*, II.4). An overly sanguine view, as we shall
see.
[194]Quigley, *Tragedy and Hope*, p. 65.
[195]*Report and Accompanying Documents of the United States Monetary Commission*,
organized under Joint Resolution of Aug. 15, 1876, 44th Cong., 2d sess., S. Rept.
703, GPO, 1877, pp. 53-54.

under the regime of deflation. The sole beneficiary was the holder of specie, whose holdings gain in value as the surrounding economy collapses. "Money in shrinking volume … is the fruitful source of political and social disturbance. It foments strife between labor and other forms of capital, while itself hidden away in security gorges on both. It rewards close-fisted lenders and filches from and bankrupts enterprising borrowers. It circulates freely in the stock exchange but avoids the labor exchange. It has in all ages been the worst enemy with which society has had to contend."[196]

The hardest hit in such a shrinking economy is the laborer, who has no property to fall back on, whose only capital is his labor. It is this which led to the pitched battle in the 19th century between capital and labor. And here the *Report* makes a most significant point: the relationship between these two is *not* foreordained to absolute conflict. It all depends on the "money-system."

> Under any money-system whatever, labor, money, and other forms of capital confront each other as opposing forces, each seeking through a natural instinct to secure as much as possible of the others in exchange. These forces, although always operating against, are not necessarily inimical to or destructive of each other. On the contrary, under a just money-system, they are not even harmful to each other…. But under an unjust money-system, under a system which through law or accident fails to regulate the quantity of money so as to preserve the equilibrium between money and the other factors of production, the conflict between money and labor and other forms of capital becomes destructive and ruinous.[197]

Indeed, how much of the rise of communism and socialism can be attributed simply to just such unjust monetary arrangements?

> It is in the shadow of a shrinking volume of money that disorders social and political gender and fester, that communism organizes, that riots threaten and destroy, that labor starves, that capital-

---

[196] *Report*, p. 53.
[197] *Report*, p. 57.

ists conspire and workmen combine, and that the revenues of governments are dissipated in the employment of laborers, or in the
maintenance of increased standing armies to overawe them. The
peaceful conflict which under a just money-system is continually
waged between money capital and labor, and which tends only to
secure the rights of each, and is essential to the progress of society,
is changed under a shrinking volume of money to an unrelenting
war, threatening the destruction of both.[198]

This was the situation under the regime of free trade combined with
the gold standard, what Polanyi referred to as the "self-regulating market."[199] With national currencies providing no buffers against the vagaries of
foreign exchange, there was simply no means to absorb shocks; growth in
one country triggered gold influxes, removing gold from other countries,
precipitating deflationary decline there; and the producing and laboring
classes bore the brunt of it.

This obviously benefitted the creditor class; but in the interest of
fairness it must be noted that not all members of this class pursued this
myopic strategy. In fact, there were big money men, financiers of the first
rank, who opposed this movement and wished to retain silver as a component of the money base, precisely because they recognized the claims of the
greater good. For example, contrary to claims made in the populist
conspiracy-oriented literature, the Rothschild bank in Paris was opposed to
the exclusive gold standard.[200] Another leading financier, Ernest Seyd, cam-
paigned against an exclusive international gold standard. Seyd displayed

---

[198]*Report*, p. 57.

[199]Karl Polanyi, *The Great Transformation: The Political and Economic Origins of
Our Time* (Boston: Beacon Press, 1944), p. 3. Because the market sets the value of
the currency, Polanyi viewed this as the market in its purest form: hence, self-regulating. But this still begs various questions, such as, how does the market choose a
currency? It is not the market but the state which, in the 19th century, chose gold.
Legal tender was still very much a part of the gold-standard regime. Hence, self-
regulation was never entirely the case. Nevertheless, Polanyi's point is well-taken:
the market did fix the value of the currency, once, of course, that currency was set
apart.

[200]On this point see Flandreau, *The Glitter of Gold*, pp. 151ff., 233-234.

Figure 17: "Take Your Choice." On the left, prosperous bimetallism; on the right, penurious monometallism, the result of demonetizing silver. From the popular pro-silver book, *Coin's Financial School* by Wm. H. Harvey (Chicago: Coin Publishing Co., 1896).

keen insight into the working of a restricted, controlled money supply. This practical understanding lends his analysis the penetration that was lacking in writers at one remove, such as Karl Marx. As Seyd clearly explained, "unless … means could be devised to compensate those who lose by this depreciation and demonetisation of Silver, and to reorganise the whole of society upon this reduced basis of value (tasks utterly impossible of accomplishment), we must face the plain patent fact that the loss suffered by property and by labour will correspondingly benefit the holder of money – the capitalist."[201] *This is the key to the entire social question of the 19th century,* and the truth behind Marx's critique.

Marx's critique of capitalism stands and falls with the concept of surplus value. What this means is that the "value-added" generated in the production process by workers is siphoned off and deposited in the accounts of those who did not work for it. But this is incomplete; for not only did workers generate surplus value, so did foremen, managers, and entre-

---

[201]Ernest Seyd, *The Depreciation of Labour and Property Which Would Follow the Demonetisation of Silver* (London: Effingham Wilson, 1869), p. 56.

preneurs. The real conflict was between producers in general and the creditor class.

A money supply based on the gold standard guarantees the flow of "surplus value" toward the holders of money and away from the producers, whether manufacturer or laborer. "It is the property of the rich as well as the labour of the poor that will have to suffer from this reduction in the world's currency, whilst the whole benefit of the operation will accrue exclusively to the capitalist alone, whose power it will increase, without any effort of his; nay, even despite any check he might himself feel inclined to oppose to the effects of this movement in his favour."[202]

It was an odd combination of banking and financial interests on the one hand and doctrinaire political economists on the other that foisted the gold-standard agenda on the nations. The free-trade regime those economists championed was hijacked by this monetary system, in the process forever sullying the name of free trade. The classical economists then (and their followers now) never quite understood the underlying rationale for opposition to their program. In their view, all of this was simply natural law, and all those suffering under it were suffering due to their own misfortune, or vice, or laziness, or some combination thereof.

Here, too, is something to give one pause: the preaching of virtue and the desire to extend "tough love" to those disadvantaged by the system. The churches were harnessed to the cause, preaching submission and resignation in the face of what boiled down to inherent injustice – along the way, giving the labor and socialist movements reason enough to embrace Marx's epithet that religion is "the opium of the people."

Seyd foresaw the direction the system would take, once the majority of nations went on gold. "We have demonstrated before that if Silver is abandoned, and Gold is made to do its office, the value of Gold must rise very considerably. England cannot escape this any more than other States; she must either part with her Gold in return for the cheapened products coming to her shores, or the price of property and labour in the country must fall in obedience to the dictates of international trade." That is, either

---

[202]Seyd, *The Depreciation of Labour and Property*, p. 56.

the banking system would come under severe stress paying for cheap imports, or domestic prices and wages would have to fall. "And, whilst thus the poor and labouring classes, as well as the holders of property, will suffer, the capitalist and the man of fixed income alone will profit (perhaps to the extent of 25 per cent.), which will give capital and fixed incomes so much the stronger hold."[203]

Such reasoning led to an ineluctable conclusion: "The single Gold valuation, the writer believes, will bring misery to the world, and the curse of posterity will fall on its advocates if they succeed in carrying their theories into practice—theories which, blind to all opposing influences and considerations, they are weak-minded enough to hold supreme."[204]

---

[203]Seyd, *The Depreciation of Labour and Property*, pp. 99-100.
[204]Seyd, *The Depreciation of Labour and Property*, p. 82.

HOARDING GOLD.

Figure 18: The critics' view of the "automatic mechanism." "Politics" holds the balance; the "financial manipulator" tips the scales in favor of gold – disparagingly characterized as "the only 'honest' money" – against commodities. From *Coin's Financial School* by Wm. H. Harvey (Chicago: Coin Financial School, 1896).

14. THE GREAT
TRANSFORMATION

The gold-based system centered on London generated instabilities and conflicts that led directly to the First World War. Everything had gone well enough, at least in terms of international relations, as long as the system itself remained unquestioned. But with the onset of the Boer War in 1899, and the adverse effect this had on public opinion in Germany, the primacy of London came under fire.

The Boer War resulted from Britain's move to annex South Africa, with its newly-discovered diamond and gold mines, at the end of the 19th century. "Boer" means "farmer" in Afrikaans, and it was indeed a war of British colonial armies versus South African citizen-farmers. But the conquest also spelled the annexation of areas (e.g., the Transvaal) in which Germans had heavily invested in previous decades. German public opinion was firmly in favor of the Boers, and Kaiser Wilhelm even sent a telegram to the leader of the Boer forces congratulating them for their obstinate resistance. But Germany could do nothing to affect events. For the entire international order, based as it was on British financial hegemony, was also based on British military hegemony, and thus the British fleet.[205]

That fleet, it was now evident, could be used not only to maintain international peace, but also to further the ends of the British empire; and Germany drew the appropriate conclusion. "Without a fleet, she thought, all colonial possessions, all overseas investments were at the mercy of the British. Hence the German naval programme, to which the British had to

---

[205]Succinctly expressed in the colonial-period anthem *Rule Britannia:*

> Rule, Britannia!
> Britannia rule the waves!
> Britons never will be slaves!

reply – the race in armaments."[206] Not only did Britain reply by embarking on an arms race, but also by building new alliances, in particular with Japan.

The trust in an implicit center had now broken down. "The financial system can only work so long as there is in the world only a single important base for foreign lending.... Up till the Boer War there was even a possibility that the German financiers would be willing to operate through the London system. The Boer War, as they thought, showed that they could not hope for fair treatment from such a system. From that moment the unity of the money-power was broken and the breakdown of its rule certain."[207]

Colonial and financial conflicts and imbalances thus led to the First World War, which, for its part, forced the nations off of strict adherence to the gold standard – there was simply no other way to generate the required financial means. Besides the physical devastation, the war produced unheard-of levels of public debt and inflation. The world was fundamentally altered. But the financial powers, which had not been dislodged, refused to recognize this simple fact. Rather, acting as if nothing had happened, they worked with might and main to restore the system that was already showing signs of unsustainable strain even before the war.

"As soon as the war was finished," writes Quigley, "governments began to turn their attention to the problem of restoring the prewar financial system. Since the essential element in that system was believed to be the gold standard with its stable exchanges, this movement was called 'stabilization.' Because of their eagerness to restore the prewar financial situation, the 'experts' closed their eyes to the tremendous changes which had resulted from the war."[208] Pursuit of the will-o'-the-wisp "stabilization" would prove the world's undoing, leading to a conflict even more devastating than the so-called "War to End All Wars" had been.

What the nations did not realize is that stabilization, even if it had worked before, would not work now. The world economic situation had changed dramatically, and not only because of the inflation and burgeoning public debt brought on by the war years. The very structure of the world

---

[206]Hollis, *The Two Nations*, p. 192.
[207]Hollis, *The Two Nations*, p. 197.
[208]Quigley, *Tragedy and Hope*, p. 320.

economy had changed fundamentally. Over the course of decades, labor had organized itself against these economic blows, increasingly gaining wage guarantees so as to avoid bearing that brunt. This, along with protectionist measures, put an ever-increasing crimp in the functioning of the automatic mechanism, as became evident in the aftermath of the First World War. "The old organization of relatively free commerce among countries specializing in different types of production was replaced," writes Quigley, "by a situation in which a larger number of countries sought economic self-sufficiency by placing restrictions on commerce." And the underdeveloped areas of the world no longer contented themselves simply with providing raw materials in exchange for the developed world's manufactured goods. They were now manufacturing their own goods, throwing them onto the world market in competition with the developed world's production. "The result was a situation where all countries were eager to sell and reluctant to buy, and sought to achieve these mutually irreconcilable ends by setting up subsidies and bounties on exports, tariffs, and restrictions on imports, with disastrous results on world trade."[209]

In the midst of this changed world, with countries shielding themselves from the adverse effects of the system of the gold standard, the financial and governmental ruling powers, preeminently Britain, attempted to maintain the old free-trade, open-borders system. It was a fool's errand, as events would prove.

Countries were no longer playing by the rules. "In an effort to stop rises in prices which might become inflationary, bankers after 1919 increasingly sought to 'sterilize' gold when it flowed into their country. That is, they sought to set it aside so that it did not become part of the monetary system. As a result, the unbalance of trade which had initiated the flow of gold was not counteracted by price changes. Trade and prices remained unbalanced, and gold continued to flow."[210] Payments imbalances were also perpetuated by bankers' action to restrict gold outflows in the face of diminishing gold reserves. "With such actions the unfavorable balance of

---

[209] Quigley, *Tragedy and Hope*, p. 322.
[210] Quigley, *Tragedy and Hope*, pp. 322-323.

trade continued, and other countries were inspired to take retaliatory actions."[211] And the changed situation regarding labor and other productive forces in society, no longer willing to shoulder the burden of imbalances, likewise served to short-circuit the automatic mechanism. "The decline in competition arising from the growth of labor unions, cartels, monopolies, and so on, made prices less responsive to flows of gold or exchange in the international markets, and, as a result, such flows did not set into motion those forces which would equalize prices between countries, curtail flows of gold, and balance flows of goods."[212]

As Quigley notes, instead of shaping a new financial arrangement adapted to these new realities, the financial powers willy-nilly attempted to restore the old system; but they had an even higher goal in mind, "nothing less than to create a world system of financial control in private hands able to dominate the political system of each country and the economy of the world as a whole." It was a system that "was to be controlled in a feudalist fashion by the central banks of the world acting in concert, by secret agreements arrived at in frequent private meetings and conferences."[213] This system was crowned by the newly-formed Bank for International Settlements (BIS), located in Basel, Switzerland, and privately owned by the various central banks. They each had accounts at the BIS, and settled accounts between themselves by bookkeeping transactions rather than actual gold shipments. "They made agreements on all the major financial problems of the world, as well as on many of the economic and political problems, especially in reference to loans, payments, and the economic future of the chief areas of the globe." Although it appeared to mark the climax of the old system, it actually constituted its siren song, an attempt to establish a control center to compensate for London's decline.[214]

---

[211]Quigley, *Tragedy and Hope,* p. 323.

[212]Quigley, *Tragedy and Hope,* p. 323.

[213]Quigley, *Tragedy and Hope,* p. 324.

[214]"The B. I. S. was a vain effort to cope with the problems arising from the growth of a number of centers. It was intended to be the world cartel of ever-growing national financial powers by assembling the nominal heads of these national financial centers." Quigley, *Tragedy and Hope,* p. 324.

During the war, with countries going off of the gold standard, domestic prices had diverged drastically from country to country. "Stabilization" required these prices to be brought back into line. This would trigger inflation in undervalued countries, deflation in overvalued countries. The US was able quickly to return to the gold standard, thanks to a favorable combination of circumstances – its newfound status as a creditor country and its position as a net exporter. Other countries did not fare so well.

> In Britain, stabilization was reached by orthodox paths – that is, taxation as a cure for public debts and deflation as a cure for inflation. These cures were believed necessary in order to go back on the old gold parity. Since Britain did not have an adequate supply of gold, the policy of deflation had to be pushed ruthlessly in order to reduce the volume of money in circulation to a quantity small enough to be superimposed on the small base of available gold at the old ratios. At the same time, the policy was intended to drive British prices down to the level of world prices. The currency notes which had been used to supplement bank notes were retired, and credit was curtailed by raising the discount rate to panic level. The results were horrible. Business activity fell drastically, and unemployment rose to well over a million and a half. The drastic fall in prices (from 307 in 1920 to 197 in 1921) made production unprofitable unless costs were driven down even faster. This could not be achieved because labor unions were determined that the burden of the deflationary policy should not be pushed onto them by forcing down wages. The outcome was a great wave of strikes and industrial unrest.[215]

After this misery, Britain was finally able to go back on the gold standard, but it did so at an overvalued pound, leading to further gold outflows. The labor unions would not submit to reduced wages to offset the deflation, and the wealthy would not submit to heavier taxation to pay the public debt. The results were abysmal: "deflation and depression for the whole period 1920-1933." Prices fell, sometimes precipitously, sometimes

---

[215]Quigley, *Tragedy and Hope*, p. 332.

gradually. Further, "the number of unemployed averaged about 1¾ millions for each of the thirteen years of 1921-1932 and reached 3 million in 1931." To add insult to injury, "the inadequacy of the British gold reserve during most of the period placed Britain in financial subjection to France (which had a plentiful supply of gold because of her different financial policy). This subjection served to balance the political subjection of France to Britain arising from French insecurity, and ended only with Britain's abandonment of the gold standard in 1931."[216]

Rather than imitate Britain, other countries devalued their currencies. These included Belgium, France, and Italy. The countries at the losing end of the war, such as Germany, resorted to hyperinflation and the destruction of their currencies. In the case of Germany, this resulted in the Dawes Plan of 1924, by which the US essentially loaned Germany the money both to rebuild its industrial plant and make reparations payments.

By 1931 a semblance of the gold standard had been restored in some 50 countries, but it was not the same gold standard as prior to the First World War. "Even in its most superficial aspects the international gold standard of 1914 was not reestablished by 1930. The legal provisions were different; the financial necessities and practices were quite different; the profound underlying economic and commercial conditions were entirely different, and becoming more so." But this did not keep the financial and political powers from pretending that this was the case. "They had created a facade of cardboard and tinsel which had a vague resemblance to the old system, and they hoped that, if they pretended vigorously enough, they could change this facade into the lost reality for which they yearned."[217]

They did this even as they pursued contradictory policies, policies that "drove this underlying reality ever farther from that which had existed in 1914," and all the while "they besought other governments to do differently. Such a situation, with pretense treated as if it were reality and reality treated as if it were a bad dream, could lead only to disaster. This is

[216]Quigley, *Tragedy and Hope*, p. 332.
[217]Quigley, *Tragedy and Hope*, p. 336.

what happened. The period of stabilization merged rapidly into a period of deflation and depression."[218]

McNair Wilson sees the Great Depression resulting from conflict between the Money Power and American manufacturers, who would not submit to the gold-standard rules of the game and allow free trade to depress wages so as to staunch gold outflows. "It soon became clear that the American industrial 'bosses' and their workpeople would offer a much stouter resistance to the Money power than that power was accustomed to encounter in any European country." The US had become the focus of the international financial system, thanks to gold inflows stemming from its creditor-nation status. But because of its tariff barrier, it did not allow the mechanism to function. This greatly distressed the financial powers. "The idea, for example, that the policy of protection should be abandoned in order to allow the debtors of American finance to pay in goods the interest on their loans was rejected with violence by American manufacturers, who asked if it was proposed to ruin them and their work people by forcing them to compete with cheap European labour. That, of course, was exactly what the Money power did propose." Not that American manufacturers were averse to foreign trade: they "were willing and anxious to export as much as possible, but they were not willing to lower the buying power of the home market (by cutting wages) in order to do so."[219]

The wonder is not that depression came when it did, but rather that it took so long to come. The delay fed the belief that the restoration of stabilization would instigate recovery. But the real reason for the delayed depression lay elsewhere. "The chief symptom of the unsoundness of the underlying economic reality – the steady fall in prices – was concealed in the later period (1925-1929) by a steady rise in security prices (which was erroneously regarded as a good sign) and by the excessive lending abroad of the United States.... This foreign lending of the United States was the chief reason why the maladjusted economic conditions could be kept concealed for so many years."[220] What now materialized was worldwide deflation.

---

[218]Quigley, *Tragedy and Hope*, p. 336.
[219]McNair Wilson, *Monarchy or Money Power*, ch. XXII.
[220]Quigley, *Tragedy and Hope*, p. 339.

The trigger was the Federal Reserve's action to raise its discount rate so as to dampen excess borrowing fueling the unrelenting stock-market rally. But rising stock prices were not indicative of the broader economy, and this restriction on credit put the brakes on economic growth. In combination with similar action by the Bank of England, it precipitated the stock market crash of autumn 1929. As a result, lending from the US to Europe stopped short. "These two events together tore away the facade which until then had concealed the fundamental maladjustments between production and consumption, between debts and ability to pay, between creditors and willingness to receive goods, between the theories of 1914 and the practices of 1928."[221]

Nor was this all. Exacerbated by such a long delay, the remedy turned out to be worse than the disease. "Production began to fall to the level of consumption, creating idle men, idle factories, idle money, and idle resources. Debtors were called to account and found deficient. Creditors who had refused repayment now sought it, but in vain. All values of real wealth shrank drastically."[222] In the wake of this economic downturn, the financial system broke down, beginning in central Europe, then England, France, and America. England was finally driven off of the gold standard in 1931.[223]

Other countries raised their tariff barriers against England to ward off its suddenly cheaper exports. The US, still on the gold standard, began experiencing gold outflows and resultant deflation. This led to a demand for liquidity, the collapse of the US banking system, the closing of the banks by executive order, and the US abandonment of the gold standard (1933).[224]

The pursuit of economic nationalism led to a drastic decline in world trade. But recovery came as countries pursued policies in line with domestic

---

[221]Quigley, *Tragedy and Hope,* p. 344.

[222]Quigley, *Tragedy and Hope,* p. 345.

[223]"Nobody told us we could do that!" A comment attributed to Tom Johnston, former parliamentary secretary for Scotland and Lord Privy Seal; see Barry Eichengreen and Peter Temin, "The Gold Standard and the Great Depression," in *Contemporary European History,* vol. 9, no. 2 (July 2000), p. 202.

[224]Quigley, *Tragedy and Hope,* pp. 345-350.

conditions. The last holdout in this regard was France, which in September 1936 ended up devaluing its currency, signaling the final breakup of the "gold bloc" of countries adhering to the gold standard, although some form of "stabilization" continued to be pursued.[225] It took World War II to complete the break with the old system.

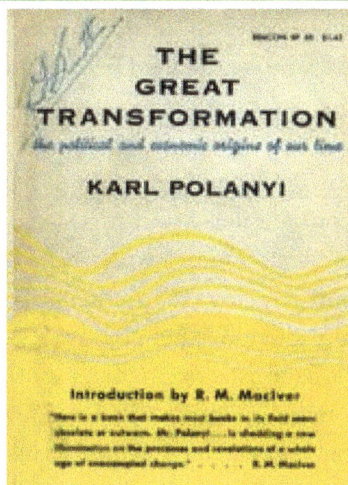

A suitably disillusioned Austrian exile by the name of Karl Polanyi in 1944 published the now-classic book highlighting the "Great Transformation" that had taken place right before his and his contemporaries' eyes. Polanyi exposed the connection between the complete collapse and restructuring of the nations, on the one hand, and the currency system on the other: for it was "the breakdown of the international gold standard" that "was the invisible link between the disintegration of world economy since the turn of the century and the transformation of a whole civilization in the thirties." And, "unless the vital importance of this factor is realized, it is not possible to see rightly either the mechanism which railroaded Europe to its doom, or the circumstances which accounted for the astounding fact that the forms and contents of a civilization should rest on so precarious foundations." This is trenchant analysis, the more so because so many around Polanyi had had no inkling of these connections. "The true nature of the international system under which we were living was not realized until it failed. Hardly anyone understood the political function of the international monetary system; the awful suddenness of the transformation thus took the world completely by surprise. And yet the gold standard was the only remaining pillar of the traditional world economy; when it broke, the effect

Figure 19: The cover of Karl Polanyi's book, *The Great Transformation*.

---

[225]Quigley, *Tragedy and Hope*, pp. 355-357.

was bound to be instantaneous." When the gold standard gave way, the dam broke that had been restraining readjustment and realignment.[226]

The countries championing the theories of the classical economists were the last to recognize this connection. "To [classical] liberal economists the gold standard was a purely economic institution; they refused even to consider it as a part of a social mechanism. Thus it happened that the democratic countries were the last to realize the true nature of the catastrophe and the slowest to counter its effects. Not even when the cataclysm was already upon them did their leaders see that behind the collapse of the international system there stood a long development within the most advanced countries which made that system anachronistic; in other words, the failure of market economy itself still escaped them." The market economy was dragged under by the failed monetary mechanism.

Many view Polanyi's book as having provided the definitive condemnation of the market economy. Indeed, Polanyi saw the Great Transformation as the result of an inherent contradiction and unsustainability in the market economy. The gold standard, in his view, had only enabled the market economy to manifest its true character. But Polanyi's analysis lends equal credence to an alternative explanation: the market economy had been hitched to a faulty monetary mechanism. When that failed, it dragged the market economy down with it.

Be that as it may, the reason the efforts to cope with the tragedy went on for so long with so little good result is because of blindness regarding the gold standard. It was the age's unifying faith, taking the place of political and religious agreement. Polanyi's litany of believers is stunning, a display of true bipartisanship.

> Belief in the gold standard was the faith of the age.... The war between heaven and hell ignored the money issue, leaving capitalists and socialists miraculously united. Where Ricardo and Marx were at one, the nineteenth century knew not doubt. Bismarck and Lassalle, John Stuart Mill and Henry George, Philip Snowden and Calvin Coolidge, Mises and Trotzky equally accepted the faith. Karl

---

[226]Polanyi, *The Great Transformation*, p. 20.

Marx had gone to great pains to show up Proudhon's utopian labor notes (which were to replace currency) as based on self-delusion; and *Das Kapital* implied the commodity theory of money, in its Ricardian form. The Russian Bolshevik Sokolnikoff was the first postwar statesman to restore the value of his country's currency in terms of gold; the German Social Democrat Hilferding imperiled his party by his staunch advocacy of sound currency principles; the Austrian Social Democrat Otto Bauer supported the monetary principles underlying the restoration of the krone attempted by his bitter opponent Seipel; the English Socialist, Philip Snowden, turned against Labor when he believed the pound sterling not to be safe at their hands; and the Duce had the gold value of the lira at 90 carved in stone, and pledged himself to die in its defense. It would be hard to find any divergence between utterances of Hoover and Lenin, Churchill and Mussolini, on this point. Indeed, the essentiality of the gold standard to the functioning of the international economic system of the time was the one and only tenet common to men of all nations and all classes, religious denominations, and social philosophies. It was the invisible reality to which the will to live could cling, when mankind braced itself to the task of restoring its crumbling existence.[227]

And when that faith collapsed, it left a yawning abyss, a seemingly unfillable vacuum. This was a fearful prospect. But waiting in the wings precisely for this moment was an obscure 18th century Scotsman, ready to take the baton, as it were, out of the palsied hand of fellow Scot Adam Smith.

---

[227]Polanyi, *The Great Transformation*, p. 25.

PART IV
THE AMERICAN
ANSWER

15. JAMES STEUART'S
COPERNICAN REVOLUTION

The post-World War II exercise in Humpty-Dumpty-like reconstruction resulted in a system bearing little resemblance to the prewar situation. Although a form of stabilization of exchange rates based on gold was established in the Bretton Woods treaty, the automatic mechanism was abandoned for good. In its place came a system centered on America and embodying principles developed in America. This was something no one had planned for. This system evolved out of actual banking practice, rather than theory. In fact, theory lagged atrociously. Having since evolved into full-fledged "best practice" across the entire world, it is a system still woefully misunderstood. Which is amazing when one considers how central it is to everything that happens at the private and public levels, locally, nationally, and internationally.

To understand this system we must retrace our steps, back to the time when the gold-based banking mechanism was being erected, to the time when mercantilist verities where being exchanged for those of classical economics. For while all of that was taking place, there was a solitary thinker busy putting together the intellectual foundations for the banking system that would eventually arise from the rubble of 19th-century boom and bust, of 20th-century world wars. Again, an astounding twist of history – for who has ever heard of James Steuart (†1780)?

Steuart, when discussed at all, is dismissed as the "last mercantilist," the foil for Adam Smith's *Wealth of Nations*.[228] Smith, of course, established

---

[228]For example: Gary M. Anderson and Robert D. Tollison, "Sir James Steuart as the Apotheosis of Mercantilism and His Relation to Adam Smith," in *Southern Economic Journal*, Vol. 51, No. 2 (Oct., 1984), pp. 456-468, in which the following statement is made: "Smith did not have to build a strawman: he had James Steuart" (p. 456). Salim Rashid disputes their conclusions in a subsequent issue of the same journal ("Smith, Steuart, and Mercantilism: Comment," Vol. 52, No. 3 [Jan., 1986], pp. 843-852).

In another article, Rashid writes of the relation between Steuart and Smith.

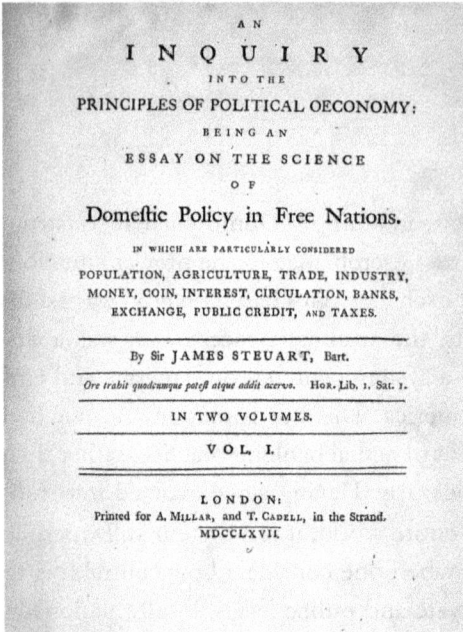

Figure 20: The title page of Sir James Steuart's seminal work, *An Inquiry Into the Principles of Political Oeconomy*, published in 1767 (MDCCLXVII).

the school of economic thought that ruled the following century, that led to so much of the misunderstanding and blindness that has afflicted subsequent economic thought and practice. As far as the analysis of money and banking is concerned, Steuart's work transcends Smith's as a BMW on the autobahn transcends a horse-drawn buggy on a rutted dirt road. And yet, we have such glittering examples of ignorance in the scientific literature as these statements by Fetter,[229] arguing that Steuart's "long discussion of banking was largely descriptive.... he gave little analysis of the economic significance of bank operations"

(p. 8), and that Adam Smith "gave the first organized analysis of banking since John Law, but showed greater familiarity with its details...." Smith was locked into the commodity-money mindset while his economics served as one of its ideological bulwarks.

"The author who could have most expected that Smith would have referred to him but who was nonetheless passed over in complete silence was Sir James Steuart. In a letter to William Pultney, Smith spoke condescendingly of Steuart's *Inquiry*, perhaps the first systematic treatise on economics in English to be laid before the public: 'I have the same opinion of Sir James Steuart's book that you have. Without once mentioning it, I flatter myself that any fallacious principle in it will meet with a clear and distinct confutation in mine.' Later Smith deepened to [sic] the wound by saying that he had not come across any intelligible account of the Bank of Amsterdam written in English, thus implying that Steuart's own description of that bank was unintelligible!" Salim Rashid, "Adam Smith's Acknowledgments: Neo-Plagiarism and the Wealth of Nations," in *Journal of Libertarian Studies*, Fall 1990, 9 (2), p. 13.

[229]Frank Whitson Fetter, *Development of British Monetary Orthodoxy 1797-1875* (Cambridge, MA: Harvard University Press, 1965).

Steuart merits the closest attention, because he managed to unlock the secrets of money and banking. Astonishingly, he revealed the workings of banking as it is practiced today, albeit in rudimentary form. As he repeatedly emphasized in his writing, and as the title of his *magnum opus* indicates, he was concerned with economic *principles,* themselves inferred from close observation of how money and banking was practiced. This allowed him to make statements of broader application and of universal validity.

Steuart worked within the parameters set by the new reality of commodity-based currency. He did not argue for a return to fiduciary coinage; in fact, he joined in the contemporary critique of that system, based as it was on varying metallic content. "Debasing the standard is odious in the opinion of every mortal,"[230] Steuart concluded. But he did not stop there. In fact, he accepted the premise only to refute the conclusion: a commodity-based currency, he argued, was inherently unstable and, indeed, anomalous.

The nature of money is to be a scale, a measure of value. The characteristic of a scale is that it measures proportions; it relates parts to the whole, while leaving to one side what, or how large, that whole might be. A scale simply takes the total of whatever is being measured and divides it up into proportional units. The relation of part to whole remains unchanged. This is what enables a scale to constitute a measure of the value, measuring ever-changing value in an unchanging way. It is this scale function that characterizes true money, what Steuart calls money of account.[231]

---

[230]Sir James Steuart, *An Inquiry into the Principles of Political Oeconomy* (London: A. Millar et al., 1767), vol. I, p. 578.

[231]"Money of account, which I shall here call *money,* performs the same office with regard to the value of things, that degrees, minutes, seconds, &c. do with regard to angles, or as scales do to geographical maps, or to plans of any kind. In all these inventions, there is constantly some denomination taken for the unit. In angles, it is the degree; in geography, it is the mile, or league; in plans, the foot, yard, or toise; in money, it is the *pound, livre, florin,* &c. The degree has no determinate length, so neither has that part of the scale upon plans which marks the unit: the usefulness of all those inventions being solely confined to the marking of proportion. Just so the unit in money can have no invariable determinate proportion to any part of value, that is to say, it cannot be fixed to perpetuity to any particular quantity of gold, silver, or any other commodity whatsoever." Steuart, *Inquiry,* vol. I, pp. 526-527. The spelling has been modernized in places.

Because the things that get valued – commodities – are constantly changing in value, no commodity is suitable to serve as money, for the very fact that it is a commodity, and thus constantly fluctuating in value. That which measures value cannot at the same time be something that receives value. Therefore, silver and gold are unsuited to serve as measures of value.

> Could gold and silver coin exactly perform the office of money, it would be absurd to introduce any other measure of value; but there are moral and physical incapacities in the metals, which prevent their performing the function of a scale: and the common opinion being, that there are no such incapacities, makes it necessary to expose them in the clearest light, by shewing the exact difference between *price* (that is coin) considered as a measure, and *price* considered as an equivalent for value. The inconsistencies which follow, when we depend blindly upon the infallibility of the metal's discharging this double office, tend to confound the whole system of our ideas concerning those matters.[232]

Coin as measure is one thing; coin as equivalent for value is another. The two cannot be combined. Because silver and gold are things, they *cannot* serve adequately as money! How can the money supply expand and contract in accordance with the rhythms of the broader economy, if it is fixed to a quantity of things that in the nature of the case never expands and contracts accordingly? And the attempt to use them as money – thus, to harness their "intrinsic value," i.e., the fact that human beings universally attach value to them – led to repeated disaster, either in the form of coinage (e.g., the Roman empire) or in the form of a commodity-based banking system (Babylon, the gold standard).

But Steuart discerned an alternative. By paying attention to evolving banking practice, in particular in his native Scotland, he noted that the key characteristic was *not* the issue of bank notes as proxies for hard-currency reserves. Steuart's great achievement was to liberate money issue from a commodity base by realizing that the essence of banking was the creation of credit on the basis of, and as a representation of, property – any kind of property, defined as a marketable asset.

---

[232]Steuart, *Inquiry*, vol. 1, p. 529.

How was money to be backed by property? By issuing bank notes and other forms of fiduciary currency against the security put up by the borrower as collateral. Such issues are not created "out of nothing," nor as receipts for specie on deposit (such deposits were never more than a fraction of the "money substitutes" issued anyway). Instead, they were created as a means of capitalizing property precisely through the mechanism of collateral. This functionality was a product of the legal system, of property and contract. Property put up for collateral had to be appraised for its value; this was already standard procedure. What Steuart realized was that this procedure in fact was the cornerstone of the entire process of money creation. It was the collateral that provided the value against which money was issued.

Steuart characterized this process as the "melting down" of property into "symbolical" money, and thus captured perfectly, for an audience steeped in the ways of metallic currency, the essence of the process. Property was made into money and yet all the while it remained property – because money is not property, is not a thing, but a representative of things in terms of a scale. If such money is nothing, then so are latitude, longitude, temperature, and the like. Money is a scale, registering capitalized property, and is issued as a component – a by-product, if you will – of credit/debt relations.

This constituted a veritable "Copernican Revolution" in monetary theory. Under fractional-reserve banking, collateral had already been required by lenders, and had usually played the role of wealth redistributor, a kind of reverse welfare, where wealth flowed into the hands of the haves at the expense of the have-nots. This is the origin of the notion, "the rich get richer while the poor get poorer." But in Steuart's system, collateral turned from a curse into a blessing.[233]

---

[233]This game-changing reversal has been integrated into a full-fledged theory of money, credit, and banking, in the works of the modern-day German economic thinkers Gunnar Heinsohn, Otto Steiger, and Hans-Joachim Stadermann. These men have rescued Steuart's seminal insight and contribution from the oblivion consigned him by the triumph of Adam Smith, David Ricardo, and the other representatives of classical economists. See the bibliography for a listing of their key works.

Steuart thus understood that the money supply comprises specie *and* the various forms of credit. These two forms he described as *real* and as *symbolical* money. "By symbolical money, I understand what is commonly called credit, or an expedient for keeping accounts of debt and credit between parties, expressed in those denominations of money which are realized in the coin. Bank notes, credit in bank, bills, bonds, and merchants' books (where credit is given and taken) are some of the many species of credit included under the term *symbolical money*."[234] These two taken together form one money supply – therefore, credit-based money comes to stand on the same footing as specie, rather than the one being considered a "money substitute" for the other. Credit-based money in this way takes its place as a full-fledged component of the money supply.

In fact, it was metallic currency that Steuart considered to be anomalous and merely an artifact. Anomalous because, as outlined above, no commodity can likewise serve as a measure of value; and an artifact, because it is the creature of custom. "In most countries in Europe (I may say all), it is customary to circulate coin, which, for many uses, is found fitter than paper (no matter for what reason); custom has established it, and with custom even statesmen must comply. The paper-money is generally made payable in coin; from custom also."[235]

The "melting down" of property into money is for Steuart the best way to obtain a circulation of a volume and quality appropriate to existing economic conditions. It is the function of banks to exercise this function. "Banking, in the age we live, is that branch of credit which best deserves the attention of a statesman. Upon the right establishment of banks, depends the prosperity of trade, and the equable course of circulation;" for "by them *solid property* may be melted down."

Steuart goes on to elucidate what he means by "solid property."

Solid property, here, is not taken in the strictest acceptation. In countries of commerce, where banks are generally established, every denomination of good personal security may be considered as solid property. Those who have personal estates, may obtain credit from

---

[234]Steuart, *Inquiry*, vol. 1, p. 365.
[235]Steuart, *Inquiry*, vol. 2, p. 170.

banks as well as landed men; because these personal estates are secured either on lands, or in the funds, or in effects which contain as
real a value as lands, and these being affected by the securities which
the proprietors grant to the bank, may with as much propriety be
said to be melted down, as if they consisted in lands. In subjects of
this nature, it is necessary to extend the meaning of our terms, in
proportion to the circumstances concerning which we reason.[236]

Good securities are the true basis of a stable and reliable money issue.

In Steuart's analysis, there are three basic forms of good securities
upon which to base the circulation: landed property, merchant's bills (bills
of exchange, accounts receivable), and public debt. These translate into
three kinds of credit: private, mercantile (or business), and public.

Where the economy is undeveloped, the best way to put it onto an
economic growth track – here Steuart sounds as if he were advising an
emerging-market country today – is to establish banks based on private
credit, thus landed property.

> In countries where trade and industry are in their infancy,
> credit can be but little known; consequently, they who have solid
> property, must find great difficulty in turning it into money; without
> money, again, industry cannot be carried on ...; consequently with-
> out credit the whole plan of national improvement will be disap-
> pointed. Under such circumstances, it is proper to establish a bank
> upon the principles of private credit. This bank must issue notes
> upon land and other securities, and the profits of it must arise from
> the permanent interest drawn for the money lent.[237]

The Scottish banking system was erected upon this basis, and subse-
quently produced the spectacular growth shown by the Scottish economy in
the 18th century. Noting this, Steuart tendered some sage advice: "To [the
Scottish banks of private credit] the improvement of this country is entirely
owing; and until they are generally established in other countries of Europe,

---

[236]Steuart, *Inquiry*, vol. 2, p. 149.
[237]Steuart, *Inquiry*, vol. 2, p. 147.

where trade and industry are little known, it will be very difficult to set these great engines to work."[238]

Such banks are just as useful in countries in which trade, industry, and circulation are developed: "Although I have represented this species of banks, which I shall call *banks of circulation upon mortgage*, as peculiarly well adapted to countries where industry and trade are in their infancy, their usefulness to all nations, who have upon an average a favourable balance upon their trade, will sufficiently appear upon an examination of the principles upon which they are established."[239]

Even so, the Bank of England answers better the purposes of the economy in England, what with its great mercantile interest and, in particular, the needs of government. For this reason, the Bank of England based its issue of currency on mercantile credit, thus the discounting of merchants' bills, and public credit, i.e., government bonds. "The ruling principle of this bank, and the ground of their confidence, is mercantile credit. The bank of England does not lend upon mortgage, nor personal security: their profits arise from discounting bills; loans to government, upon the faith of taxes, to be paid within the year; and upon the credit cash of those who deal with them. A bank such as that of England, cannot therefore be established, except in a great wealthy mercantile city, where the accumulation of the smallest profits amount, at the end of the year, to very considerable sums."[240]

What is striking is that nowhere does Steuart make convertibility into specie a defining characteristic of these banks. For Steuart, these banks did not extend credit on the supposition that every issue was backed by specie deposit. They extended credit simply on the basis of good securities, thus qualifying property encumbered as collateral; and in the case of the Bank of England, specie is also required to maintain the balance of payments with foreign countries. In effect, Steuart was waving the specie-based money supply good-bye.

---

[238]Steuart, *Inquiry*, vol. 2, p. 147.
[239]Steuart, *Inquiry*, vol. 2, p. 147.
[240]Steuart, *Inquiry*, vol. 2, p. 148.

16. THE AMERICAN FACE OF STEUART

The 13 North American English colonies grew up during the time England was moving toward the gold standard, and thus had to deal with currency scarcity. This had an even more deleterious effect in the colonies that it did in England, for only the best American customers – plantation owners and merchants – had access to the specie required for commercial relations with English merchant counterparts. The less well-to-do colonists had to make do with the opportunities and products yielded by the as-yet undeveloped domestic economy, with its makeshift currencies.

The great need of the colonies economically was a functioning indigenous currency allowing for broad participation in economic activity. But the mercantilist system as practiced by England most definitely subordinated this domestic need to the desire on the part of English merchants to maintain the colonists' dependency upon English manufactures. To pay for those manufactures, the colonists had to export raw materials – a classic case of a colonial center-periphery arrangement. These exports were not enough to cover the costs, leading to a trade deficit. Hence, specie gravitated to the mother country. A colonial domestic currency would foment indigenous manufacturing, undercutting the relationship with the mother country. Therefore, the mother country maintained control of the money supply and cut down on these indigenous expedients, for its own benefit.

Although one of the major strands of colonial history, the condition of the currency has been neglected by historians – when not totally misrepresented by them. Nineteenth-century historians under the spell of the gold standard castigated the colonists for introducing fiduciary forms of currency, characterizing them as profligate debtors out to fleece honest merchants. This is the stereotype, and it needs drastic revision.[241]

Alexander Del Mar was one of the first to undertake such a revision. "Few events have occurred in the history of mankind of more general im-

---

[241]Hammond's discussion is particularly helpful in this regard: see *Banks and Politics in America*, pp. 12ff, 30ff. This book won the Pulitzer Prize for history in 1958.

portance than the American Revolution," he wrote. "It was not merely the assertion of independent sovereignty by a few remote and obscure colonies. It was the establishment of an order of society which had been substantially forgotten for eighteen centuries; it was the separation of Church and State, and the extinction of the feudal system, and that too among a people with such natural advantages and opportunities of growth and progress, that this new order of affairs was likely to create a new empire, greater than that of all Europe." Such a new community "demanded the establishment of institutes favourable to its rapid development and the removal of such institutes as threatened to retard or prevent it."[242]

One such institution was money, "imposed upon it by the Mercantile system of Great Britain. This system encouraged the import and discouraged the export of the precious metals from England. Therefore, unless the North American Colonies could produce these metals from their own soil, which happily for posterity they could not" (countries that did generate precious metals, such as Spain, never seemed to benefit from them but rather suffered over the long term) "they had to be contented with such money as the Crown chose to provide them with." Nevertheless, the lack of an indigenous money supply combined with the mother country's abstemious monetary policy constituted a serious problem. "It is evident that with money, the supplies of which were subject to the power of a distant sovereign and an apathetic ministry, the orderly development of the Colonies was impossible, and hence followed those efforts to establish at first a silver coinage and afterwards a paper system of their own, which led to the contentions between them and the Crown that distinguished the latter half of the 17th and first half of the 18th century." Thus, this conflict over currency was one of the main contributing factors to the Revolution. "When in 1774 [sic] the Act was promulgated which required a stamp to be place [sic] upon every instrument of commerce, and thus threatened to suppress or defeat that restoration of the paper money system which was at that time being sought, the bitterness of the Colonists grew to phrenzy and resulted in

---

[242]Alexander Del Mar, *The History of Money in America from the Earliest Times to the Establishment of the Constitution* (New York: The Cambridge Encyclopedia Company, 1899), pp. 93-94.

those acts of resistance to the Crown which have been dignified by the names of the 'battles' of Lexington and Concord."[243]

The colonies had attempted all manner of expedients to alleviate the shortage of currency. Colonial governments would issue temporary payment notes that they would accept in payment of taxes. Government land offices were established by which landed property was "melted down," to use Steuart's phrase, into currency. In Virginia, receipts of warehoused tobacco were used. And the hard currency in circulation was usually foreign. The main coin used was the Spanish dollar, also known as the piece of eight (see figure 21). The silver dollar of the new American nation would be based on this coin.[244]

Figure 21: Spanish dollar, Potosí mint, under Carlos III (1768). Source: Classical Numismatics Group, Inc. http://www.cngcoins.com

In English eyes, banks were a problem. Attempts to establish them, on the basis of Steuartian principles of solid property, were met with Parliamentary legislation banning them altogether, a rather odd procedure considering that they were allowed, at least in restricted fashion, in the mother country as well as in Scotland. But the underlying rationale is clear: the colonies needed to be kept in a dependent condition.

Government-issued paper money fared better – championed by no less illustrious a figure than Benjamin Franklin, who, being a printer himself, developed ingenious anti-counterfeiting measures for his own issues.[245] Pennsylvania, where Franklin's issues were conducted, had a good reputation for currency of integrity, while other colonies, such as Rhode Island, did not. But the Currency Act of 1751 put a damper on this activity, at least

---

[243] Alexander Del Mar, *The History of Money in America*, p. 94.

[244] It is surmised that the dollar sign ($) was derived from one of the pillars-with-ribbon as depicted on the reverse of the piece of eight.

[245] Such as the imprinting of the vein patterns of actual leaves, which were unreproducible in detail. See figure 22.

Figure 22: Bill of credit issued by Benjamin Franklin and D. Hall, 1760. Source: http://www.metamute.org/editorial/articles/bitcoin-%E2%80%93-finally-fair-money

in New England.[246] The ban was extended to all the colonies by means of a second Currency Act, this one in 1764, mandating that "no act, order, resolution, or vote of assembly, in any of his Majesty's colonies or plantations in America, shall be made, for creating or issuing any paper bills, or bills of credit of any kind or denomination whatsoever."[247]

The bad blood this engendered was overshadowed by other, more notorious acts of the British government, such as the Stamp Act of 1765. And many colonists were no more enamored of paper money than were the English.[248] But these seem mainly to have been those – plantation owners and merchants – with direct connection to English merchants. This explains the aversion to both paper money

---

[246]As indicated by the title: "An Act to regulate and restrain Paper Bills of Credit in his Majesty's Colonies or Plantations of *Rhode Island* and *Providence* Plantations, *Connecticut*, the *Massachusets Bay*, and *New Hampshire* in *America;* and to prevent the same being legal Tenders in Payments of Money." The entire act can be consulted at http://etext.lib.virginia.edu/users/brock/curract1751.htm.

[247]The act is available for perusal at:
http://avalon.law.yale.edu/18th_century/curency_act_1764.asp.

[248]The Currency Act "was coupled in spirit with the Stamp Act, the Quartering Act, and Parliament's other assumptions of power to legislate for British subjects in America without allowing them representation. These violations of constitutional rights formerly defended by the British authorities affronted the Americans more than refusal to let them have paper money and make it legal tender, which was something that many of them did not wish to do anyway." Hammond, *Banks and Politics in America*, p. 26.

and banks by such figures as Thomas Jefferson, who couched that aversion in high-sounding moralizing about the virtues of thrift, avoidance of debt, and honest money.

The issue of paper money was an overture of rebellion. "Almost the first act of the Massachusetts and the Continental revolutionary assemblies was the emission of paper money in the teeth of the Royal prerogative, and this was done while yet the Colonies had no fixed determination of separating from the mother country. Indeed, barring Lexington and Concord, which were mere skirmishes to protect some trumpery stores, the emission of paper money was the first act of open resistance and defiance which the American Colonies offered to the Crown."[249]

During the war itself, the issue of paper money evolved from act of defiance to dire necessity, and for a while it did the job it was called on to do, even Jefferson recognizing the service hereby rendered. "Considering the paper money issued by Congress in the Revolution and the paper money since issued by banks, [Jefferson] averred: 'The object of the former was a holy one; for if ever there was a holy war, it was that which saved our liberties and gave us independence. The object of the latter is to enrich swindlers at the expense of the honest and industrious part of the nation.'"[250] But overissue eventually caught up with it, bringing its value down to nothing. Still, Berkey's point is well-taken: "That a paper currency, issued to an excessive amount, by thirteen sparsely settled colonies, in a state of rebellion, under a revolutionary government possessing only a shadow of authority, against the most powerful nation on the earth, should have circulated at all, is one of the most remarkable facts connected with the Revolution, and is to be accounted for only by the patriotism of those engaged in that memorable struggle.... It circulated for over a year at par with silver, and in 1778, three years after the first emission, it depreciated only to $1.75 for $1."[251]

---

[249]Del Mar, *History of Money in America,* p. 94.
[250]Hammond, *Banks and Politics in America,* p. 196. The Jefferson quotation is from a letter to John W. Eppes, dated 6 November 1813.
[251]William A. Berkey, *The Money Question: The Legal Tender Paper Monetary System of the United States* (Grand Rapids, MI: W.W. Hart, 1876), pp. 116-117.

But thereafter its value dwindled to nothing. "Not worth a continental" became a byword for worthlessness, the continental being the name given the money issued by authority of the Continental Congress. This experience certainly was grist to the mill of gold-standard-imbued historians of later generations, but not to the new nation. "The depreciation of Continental and state-issued bills of credit has received much study, partly because Article I, Section 10 of the Constitution forbid [sic] states from coining money, emitting bills of credit, or making anything but gold and silver coin a tender in payment of debts. While true that the wartime depreciation led to those stimulations, the frequent assertion that the experience soured Americans on paper money is incorrect."[252] What did sour Americans on paper money was government-issued legal tender; in its place came bank-issued notes. The new nation would be built on the principles enunciated by James Steuart, whereby banks of circulation, generating credit on the basis of good securities – melting property into symbolical money – provided the liquidity needed by a burgeoning economy impatient of the artificial restrictions imposed by a rigid metallic-currency requirement.

American growth boomed after the Revolution, in the process transforming the new nation unrecognizably. All the while, Americans, consistent with the mind-set of the age, continued to pay lip-service to the ideal of specie convertibility. It was this characteristic of bank notes – that they might be converted into specie at any time – that led men like Thomas Paine to prefer them to government-issued paper. "Bank notes are of a very different kind, and produce a contrary effect. They are promissory notes payable on demand, and may be taken to the bank and exchanged for gold or silver without the least ceremony or difficulty.... [Government] Paper money appears, at first sight, to be a great saving, or rather that it costs nothing; but it is the dearest money there is."[253] But to others, such specie convertibility was an obvious sham; opponents railed against it, albeit to

---

[252]Robert E. Wright, *Origins of Commercial Banking in America, 1750-1800* (Lanham, MD: Rowman & Littlefield Publishers, Inc., 2001), p. 85.

[253]Thomas Paine, *Dissertations on Government*, in Nancy B. Spannaus and Christopher White, eds., *The Political Economy of the American Revolution* (Washington, D.C.: Executive Intelligence Review, 1996), pp. 321-322; quoted in Wright, *Origins of Commercial Banking*, pp. 86-87.

Figure 23: An example of early American banking exuberance. A five-dollar bank-note issued by the Erie & Kalamazoo Rail Road Bank in 1853. The portrait is of President Franklin Pierce. Source: Michael Holley via Wikimedia Commons.

little effect. John Adams, for one, seethed that "every dollar of a bank bill that is issued beyond the quantity of gold and silver in the vaults represents nothing and is therefore a cheat upon somebody."[254]

Lip service turned serious, however, when the stipulation for specie convertibility actually began to be enforced by budding central bankers desirous of putting the brakes on exuberant growth – or fearful of rising prices, the bane of creditors everywhere. The Second Bank of the United States (SBUS) was formed in the wake of the War of 1812 as an instrument to help restore government finances. In the 1820s, it began acting as a sort of central bank: Nicholas Biddle, the bank's director, can even lay claim to being a pioneer in the field. The bank was able to do this by taking advantage of the fact that bullion was still the only "real" money. Because of this, banks had to maintain a reserve of specie in order to meet any claim for conversion of notes into specie. The SBUS would take the notes of the various banks received in deposit from e.g. the Treasury Department from tax revenues, and present them to those banks in exchange for specie. This kept the banks "honest" and restrained them from lending too much above and beyond their specie reserves. The SBUS was able to do this effectively because it received copious amounts of deposits from the various sources of tax revenue – largely paid in other banks' notes – and because it had

---

[254]Quoted in Hammond, *Banks and Politics in America*, p. 196.

branches spread across the country. Because the banking system was organized by and within the states, not the Union, this kept other banks from
developing a similar, national branch structure.

Opposition to the SBUS and its restrictive policy reached the boiling
point during the administration of Andrew Jackson (1828-1836), famous for
the "Bank War" in which his administration challenged and defeated the
controversial central bank. Ostensibly, this "war" was fought in the name of
"the largely rural, small-business, lower-class southern and western support-
ers of Jackson in 1834," against "the bankers, financiers, big business, and
urban upper classes of the East and Northeast."[255] In all actuality, however,
it was the big banking interests, especially in the Northeast (read: New
York), who were opposed to the activity of the SBUS, as it restricted their
lending activities and overall freedom of action. Hence, Jackson's war
against the SBUS actually furthered the interests of the banking elite.

The Jackson administration's friendliness to the banking interest was
further revealed in the switch to a 16/1 silver-to-gold mint ratio in 1836.
Yet another of history's choice ironies! For Andrew Jackson to this day is
viewed as the champion of the people against the banking interest; but in
fact he inaugurated the chain of events by which that banking interest was
able to gain hegemony over the US economy.

---

[255]Milton Friedman, "The Crime of 1873," in *Journal of Political Economy*, Vol.
98, No. 6 (Dec., 1990), pp. 1162-1163.

17. GILDED AGE

The shift to a 16/1 mint ratio in 1836 tilted the specie balance in favor of gold. America hereby joined the "gold club," at least in principle, for it would not be until 1873 that the definitive step in that direction would be taken. But the trend was clear. Gold was asserting its hold over the minds of men. Increasingly it was felt that only gold could anchor the international trade regime. In the minds of foreign investors, gold had become the go-to currency. They viewed the international gold standard as the only reliable way to maintain values of investment in far-flung areas where security and control became more tenuous, where law and order was in the hands of foreign powers. And the 19th century was one of the great ages of expanding globalization.

Prior to 1836, the US was on a silver standard. This was not the original intention. In his bank recommendations of 1792, Alexander Hamilton had championed a bimetallist regime of both gold and silver. Hamilton reasoned that a bimetallic regime would provide the broadest basis for banking and currency, minimizing the effect of scarcities of metal. This system was adopted, and it enabled America to avoid the artificial dependence on gold that England had imposed upon itself through its *de facto* tilt toward a gold currency. But Hamilton's recommended mint ratio of 15/1 actually worked against gold and in favor of silver.

This changed in 1836. Although the effect was not as radical as in England, economic development did experience turbulence such as the Panic of 1837, where the requirement to pay for government lands in hard currency, along with the legislative requirement that Treasury specie reserves be distributed across the various states rather than be located in centra like New York, precipitated a severe credit crunch.[256]

The shift to gold coincided with a massive change in the economic panorama and the advent of transportation on an entirely new scale. Rail-

---

[256]On the Panic of 1837, see Peter L. Rousseau, "Jacksonian Monetary Policy, Specie Flows, and the Panic of 1837," in *The Journal of Economic History*, Vol. 62, No. 2 (Jun., 2002), pp. 457-488.

roads, steamships, and channels such as the Erie Canal opened new vistas for broad economic development. However, these opportunities also required massive levels of investment on a long-term basis. For the United States, a major source of such investment came from overseas. This fed the bias toward gold; but it also made the international financial framework more fragile. The focus on gold narrowed the base upon which the system was erected, making it more susceptible to tottering.

Beginning in 1848, the gold bias received a rude shock. Gold was discovered in California and Australia. Why was this problematic? Because, all of a sudden, it appeared as if the fresh influx of gold would undermine its capacity to retain and store value. And this was of paramount importance to the gold interest: the scarcity of the metal guaranteed its value, and control of its market.

Michel Chevalier, an eminent French economist of the mid-19th century, compared the effect to the Great Inflation following the discovery of America by the Spaniards. "In our day we seem destined, like our fathers of three centuries ago, and from the same causes, to witness the spectacle, or in other words the shock and crisis, of a universal rise in prices...."[257] It seems incongruous, but it makes perfect sense given the gold-standard mentality: a sudden surge in gold supplies was seen as an onerous development. "Under the influence of this greatly increased and cheapened production of gold, it is reasonable to expect, at least in all those countries where gold circulates in large quantities, and where it is or tends to be the sole medium of exchange, a general disturbance of prices, a deeply felt derangement of interests, and a modification more or less radical in the different relations of society."[258] All of this is an indication of the mind-set of the times, which apotheosized gold. The reality was this: regardless of the benefit to the nation as a whole, an abundance of gold was seen as detrimental, simply because it was detrimental to the specie-holding creditor class. Apparently, only this class counted.

---

[257]Michel Chevalier, *On the Probable Fall in the Value of Gold: the Commercial and Social Consequences Which May Ensue, and the Measures Which it Invites,* trans. Richard Cobden (New York: D. Appleton & Co., 1859), pp. 18-19.
[258]Chevalier, *On the Probable Fall,* p. 20.

In the event, the massive inflation predicted by Chevalier did not materialize. The influx of gold in fact brought relief to beleaguered Western economies. Just in time – for the "revolution year" of 1848 might otherwise have turned into the revolution decade (1848 was as much the result of economic distress as anything else). Fresh supplies of gold brought the return of calm, the restoration of governmental authority, and a period of relative peace and progress in the nations of the Europe.

Although the discovery and increase in gold circulation had brought peace and progress to Europe, civil war was brewing in America. The war would likewise constitute a blow to the forces of gold. For in order to finance the costs of war, the Union government moved the currency entirely off of specie, whether gold or silver, and instituted the notorious "Greenback": paper currency. This currency arrangement functioned surprisingly well. Nevertheless, "at the close of the Civil War, the Administration, Congress, and the public at large were all generally committed to resumption of specie payments, and regarded contraction of the currency as a necessary step toward that end." This bias toward restoration quickly lost steam, however: "the sharp decline in prices and the business contraction that followed the end of the Civil War produced, after some lag, a marked change in sentiment."[259] Substantial numbers were catching on to the idea that economic growth depended upon a money supply capable of expanding in line with growth, and that contraction, while favorable to creditors, was devastating to producers and laborers. "Needless to say," note Friedman and Schwarz, "public controversy continued." Friedman and Schwarz's summation reveals the hardening of the battle lines: "Currency contraction was strongly advocated as a step toward immediate resumption, especially by persons engaged in foreign trade, eastern bankers, and some manufacturers, predominantly New England textile men. Currency expansion was just as strongly advocated, to offset the baleful effects of deflation, by an even more mixed lot – agrarian groups that had initially been strong proponents of currency contraction, spokesmen for labor groups, western

---

[259]Milton Friedman and Anna Jacobsen Schwartz, *A Monetary History of the United States, 1857-1960* (Princeton: Princeton University Press, 1963), pp. 44-45.

merchants and bankers, Pennsylvania ironmasters, and businessmen with interests in western real estate and transportation."[260]

The steps required to realize resumption of the dollar at the prewar parity with gold were initiated by the notorious "Crime of 1873." Buried in legislation signed by President Ulysses Grant (who later claimed he had no idea that this provision was in the bill), silver was demonetized for good.[261] The dollar-gold link was officially reestablished in 1879 when the Specie Resumption Act of 1875 took effect.

Friedman draws the remarkable parallels between the course of events in the US and the one that led to the establishment of the gold standard in England a half-century earlier:

> The events culminating in resumption in 1879 precisely parallel a corresponding sequence in Britain six decades earlier: a bimetallic standard before 1797 followed by the adoption of an inconvertible paper standard, the demonetization of silver in 1816, and resumption in 1819 on a gold basis (without the 1816 legislation, resumption would have been on silver). The parallelism is not pure coincidence. The initial step – ending convertibility and adopting a paper standard – was a reaction in both countries to the financial pressures of war. As in the United States, Britain's decision to return to a specie standard reflected the desire to have a "sound money" and the outrage of the financial community, holders of government bonds, and some economists at the inflation produced by the departure from a specie standard. Though Britain's choice of gold instead of silver for this purpose was something of an accident, it was a major reason why the United States made the same choice roughly 60 years later.[262]

---

[260]Friedman and Schwarz, *A Monetary History of the United States*, pp. 45-46.

[261]The affair and its consequences are summarized in Milton Friedman, "The Crime of 1873," in *Journal of Political Economy*, Vol. 98, No. 6 (Dec., 1990), pp. 1159-1194.

[262]Friedman, "The Crime of 1873," p. 1164.

We may beg to differ with Friedman on the question as to whether Britain's "choice" for gold was an accident. Publicly it might appear that way, but, as we have seen, behind the scenes it was deliberately pursued.

Internationally, a similar trend was under way. For fifty years, France, not England, was the anchor of the international currency system. It anchored the bimetallist silver-gold regime of which the United States, among many others, formed part. With its bimetallic standard mediating between both gold and silver countries, France formed the pivot of the international monetary regime; through its mint rate of 15.5/1 it maintained this parity between gold and silver over the entire period up until the breakup in 1873.[263]

What happened then was fateful: the Franco-Prussian War. Prussia extorted a gold-financed war indemnity from France of such magnitude that it enabled the newly united Germany to switch from silver to gold. Subsequent efforts by Germany to dump its suddenly-redundant silver, intended to inflict further damage on France, caused France to depart from the silver side of its bimetallic regime. With France and Germany now both on gold, other countries were forced to follow suit. By 1880, most of the world was on the gold standard, and England's automatic mechanism was in full swing.

The shift to a single standard made the economic history of the United States in the late 19th century schizophrenic. On the one hand there was astounding expansion of the industrial base, massive growth in transportation and communications, the conquest and integration of an entire continent – and on the other hand, unheard-of levels of misery and impoverishment through boom-bust cycles that make the experiences of the latter 20th and early 21st centuries seem walks in the park.

This was not simply due to the lack of the range of provisions to alleviate poverty, such as those sported by the modern welfare state, but to

---

[263] An eye-opening account of this hitherto grossly neglected phenomenon is contained in Flandreau, *The Glitter of Gold*.

Figure 24. New York in the Gilded Age: Mr. and Mrs. Goodhue Livingston and Mrs. Alfred Vanderbilt, 1890. Source: Wikimedia Commons.

the whipsaw nature of the business cycle and the amplitude of the swings that the cycle underwent. All of this became more pronounced as the US went onto the gold standard during the 1870s, as the automatic mechanism centered in London decreed rises and falls in interest rates, inflation and deflation, job growth and job losses, prosperity and poverty. Devastating depressions punctuated the system's progression: 1873, 1893, and 1907 being the most noteworthy, all of which had to do with gold availability or the lack thereof. The vaunted stability touted by the gold standard's adherents too often turned out to be exchange-rate stability at the expense of national prosperity, and it is no wonder that the various progressivist movements took wing at this time, not to mention the more radical variants – anarchism, socialism, and communism. All had to do with the hammerlock of the gold standard and its custodians, the private bankers, on the financial condition of nations, whether at the public level or the private.

In 1873, Mark Twain and Charles Dudley Warner published a novel entitled *The Gilded Age,* a portrayal of the corruption and venality of the post-Civil War period. The book's title was soon put to service as a description of the entire late 19th century. And indeed, a better metaphor for the period could hardly be devised. For this was certainly a gilded age: of base material overlaid with gold to give it the appearance of substance and worth. The gold standard had the appearance of stability and solidity; but it was a thin veneer. The reality was an unstable, erratic succession of frothiness and flatness, of riches and rags. This was no *golden* age, the pretension notwithstanding.

18. FROM SCARCITY
TO ABUNDANCE

Monetary policy in the wake of World War II was the unwitting brainchild of Franklin D. Roosevelt. A hodgepodge of Keynesianism and monetarism, we might term it Monetarist Keynesianism. This was seen clearly by Quigley, who castigated Roosevelt's policy precisely because it was not pure Keynesianism, but instead relied upon the central bank's monetizing debt. Quigley saw this as a continuation of "orthodox policy," when what was needed was "unorthodox policy," i.e., direct government money creation. Hence: "For the whole twelve years he was in the White House, Roosevelt had statutory power to issue fiat money in the form of greenbacks printed by the government without recourse to the banks. This authority was never used. As a result of such orthodoxy, the depression's symptoms of idle resources were overcome only when the emergency of the war in 1942 made it possible to justify a limitless increase in the national debt by limitless borrowing from private persons and the banks."[264] In other words, money was the limiting factor that led to all the calamities up to and including the Great Depression, and governments needed to take the bull by the horns and simply create it.

The New Deal did not do this: it took orthodox monetary policy, i.e., debt-based currency, and wedded it to unorthodox fiscal policy, i.e., government spending in lieu of an absence of private sector consumption and investment. For Quigley, this was the reason for its failure. The Roosevelt administration was not radical enough in its approach, because it failed to recognize the depth of the problem. "This failure can be seen in Roosevelt's theory of 'pump priming.' He sincerely believed, as did his secretary of the Treasury, that there was nothing structurally wrong with the economy, that it was simply temporarily stalled, and would keep going of its own powers if it could be restarted. In order to restart it, all that was needed, in New Deal theory, was a relatively moderate amount of government spending on a

---

[264]Quigley, *Tragedy and Hope*, p. 534.

temporary basis." From this would come purchasing power, which would reignite investor confidence, leading to productive investment and renewed economic growth.[265]

> The inadequacy of this theory of the depression was shown in 1937 when the New Deal, after four years of pump priming and a victorious election in 1936, stopped its spending. Instead of taking off, the economy collapsed in the steepest recession in history. The New Deal had to resume its treatment of symptoms but now without hope that the spending program could ever be ended, a hopeless prospect since the administration lacked the knowledge of how to reform the system or even how to escape from borrowing bank credit with its mounting public debt, and the administration lacked the courage to adopt the really large-scale spending necessary to give full employment of resources. The administration was saved from this impasse by the need for the rearmament program followed by the war.[266]

Pace Quigley, the problem was *not* government spending financed by debt instead of pure fiat currency. Rather, it was government spending as a substitute for private investment. The situation was only turned around with the coming of World War II, when government spending – *mirabile dictu* – was directed to something government actually *is* capable of achieving, viz., victory in war. If the Allies had lost, there would have been no enduring recovery.

Be that as it may, Quigley's insight cuts through a mess of verbiage, enabling us to focus our discussion on what matters: actual policy, pursued to a certain end (viz., unorthodox fiscal policy), and conducted via a certain means (viz., orthodox monetary policy). This construct serves to frame the entire postwar experience, because the policy Roosevelt patched together in the chaotic trial-and-error conditions of the 1930s is the policy that became the norm in the postwar world. Nevertheless, it was only government policy; the broader economy, and banking system, followed its own course.

---

[265]Quigley, *Tragedy and Hope*, pp. 534-535.
[266]Quigley, *Tragedy and Hope*, p. 535.

The reigning theoretical construct focuses on public (government) debt as money base, which is consistent with its government-centered approach to understanding the way things work. It thus loses sight of the other two forms of money creation as put forward by Steuart – mercantile/business credit, and mortgage loans. These latter two far outstrip public debt as money generators. Nevertheless, the central bank and its public debt monetization monopolizes the attention of market players, a fact that demonstrate the power ideas have over practice.

Keynesianism (government-created money supply) essentially constitutes an attempt to replace specie-based banking through the imitation of the regime of coinage. With a coinage regime, the state controls the money supply through its mint policy. Thus, money is created by the mint, credit expansion plays a secondary role, and banking is a restricted affair. It is this characteristic of centralized, state-oriented control of the money supply that Keynesianism attempts to recreate. It is sustained in this effort by an understanding of the shortcomings of the bullion-based system, in which private bankers centralized control of the money supply. It offers an alternative to this failed system.

For its part, monetarism (central-bank created money supply) maintains the fractional-reserve banking system but replaces specie with central-bank-issued money, called "hot money" or "high-powered money." Because the rest of the banking system has to hold some dictated level of reserves in the form of this "hot money," monetarists consider it to have some sort of metaphysical quality lacking in deposits created by other banks, even though in essence there is no difference between the two. Monetarists believe that by manipulating the "quantity" of "hot money" they can expand and contract the money supply. The only problem is that the "broader" money supply does not oblige them by expanding and contracting accordingly. The current situation of low prices and low economic activity despite central banks' fevered attempts to generate inflation is an indication that monetarism does not quite fit the facts.

Both these alternatives lose sight of the fact that in the post-gold-standard banking system, the money supply is produced in terms of the Steuartian trinity: government debt, mercantile/business credit, and mortgage lending.

Since the days of 1000%-plus inflation rates in countries like Brazil and Argentina, inflation that was financed by direct government printing of money, pure Keynesianism has lost favor. Across the world, the money supply is being left to the banking system. And because the assets upon which the money supply is generated are dispersed, efforts by central banks to control the money supply – as, for example, recent rounds of "quantitative easing" by the Federal Reserve – simply miss the point, and are either misguided (something which is hard to believe) or done for show (something which is entirely possible).[267]

If neither of these adequately explain the reality, what does? Experience showed that, with the decline of coinage and the advent of fractional-reserve banking, it was banks that were creating the money supply. This was ostensibly an extension of specie holdings, but in reality – as Steuart so presciently noted – it was occurring *not* by basing money issue on cash holdings, but on borrowers' assets: "melting" property into "symbolical" money. Bank reserves were not the base for an extended amount of money substitutes; money was actually being created, against good securities, apart from consideration of reserves.

The noted US economist Irving Fisher, professor of political economy at Yale University, pointed out this character of the banking system. "When the uninitiated first learn that the number of dollars which note holders and depositors have the right to draw out of a bank exceeds the number of dollars in the bank, they are apt to jump to the conclusion that there is nothing behind the notes or deposit liabilities. Yet behind all these obligations there is always, in the case of a solvent bank, full value; if not actual dollars, at any rate, *dollars' worth of property*." This was also Steuart's point. It is not reserves, but property put up as security, that determines the solvency of the bank. "This *true* value of the liabilities will rest upon and be equal to the *true* value of the assets behind them by means of which they will be paid, so far as may be," and these assets were not limited to cash

---

[267]The additional amount of debt monetized by the central bank in such efforts adds but little to the total money supply, and thus has minimal effect on it. Of course, in the specific case of quantitative easing the Fed was buying mortgage loans rather than public debt, in an effort to influence long-term interest rates. Such an objective is more in line with what the Fed can actually accomplish.

holdings. Property encumbrances were likewise assets. In Fisher's time, banking orthodoxy decreed that the main form of property to be used for this purpose was commercial paper – merchants' notes – "although, so far as the principles here discussed are concerned, they might be any property whatever." Behind the commercial paper of businessmen lies concrete assets, property, of all sorts, "grain, machines, and steel ingots," whatever. "The bank finds itself with liabilities which exceed its *cash* assets; but this excess of liabilities is balanced by the possession of other assets than cash. These other assets of the bank are the liabilities of business men. These liabilities are in turn supported by the assets of the business men. If we continue to follow up the chain of liabilities and assets, we shall find the ultimate basis of the bank's liabilities in the concrete tangible wealth of the world." The property base of bank credit, thus money, could not be better articulated.[268]

Fisher brings his discussion to a climax in a burst of Steuartian prose:

> This ultimate basis of the entire credit structure is kept out of sight, but the basis exists. Indeed, we may say that banking, in a sense, causes this concrete, tangible wealth to circulate. If the acres of a landowner or the iron stoves of a stove dealer cannot circulate in literally the same way that gold dollars circulate, yet the landowner or stove dealer may give to the bank a note on which the banker may base bank notes or deposits; and these bank notes and deposits will circulate like gold dollars. Through banking, he who possesses wealth difficult to exchange can create a circulating medium based upon that wealth. He has only to give his note, for which, of course, his property is liable, get in return the right to draw, and lo! his comparatively unexchangeable wealth becomes liquid currency. To put it crudely, deposit banking is a device for coining into dollars land, stoves, and other wealth not otherwise generally exchangeable.[269]

---

[268]Irving Fisher, *Elementary Principles of Economics* (New York: the Macmillan Company, 1913), pp. 172-173.
[269]Fisher, *Elementary Principles*, p. 173.

This is close to plagiarism, for Fisher nowhere gives Steuart credit for this notion of "coining" property into dollars. But it is the same as Steuart's notion of "melting down" property into money.

Therefore, what sets the banking system apart from other forms of enterprise is this capacity to create money. This was already recognized by the Scottish economist Henry Dunning Macleod, who in the mid-19th century turned the world of classical economics upside-down by introducing credit and debt into the framework of exchange. "At the present time Credit is by far the most gigantic species of Property in this country, and the trade in Debts is beyond all comparison, the most colossal branch of commerce.... The merchants who trade in Debts—namely Bankers—are now the Rulers and Regulators of Commerce: they almost control the fortunes of States. As there are shops for dealing in bread, in furniture, in clothes, and every other species of property; so there are shops, some of the most palatial structures of modern times, for the express purpose of dealing in Debts: and these shops are called Banks."[270]

The business of banks, then, is the trade in debts; and it is this trade upon which it bases its unique functionality, that of creating money. Thus, banking is not the brokering of relations between borrowers and lenders, whereby money deposited by person A is lent out to person B, with the difference in interest rates being the source of bankers' profit. Banking proper is something entirely different than this prosaic state of affairs. "The business of banking does not consist, as is so commonly supposed, and as stated in books and documents which might be supposed to be of authority, in borrowing money from one set of persons and lending it out to another set: but in creating and issuing Circulating Rights of Action, Credits or Debts, on a given basis of bullion, several times exceeding the basis: according to the different degrees of perfection on which the system is organised." (It can be seen here that Macleod is still wedded to the specie basis of money, but this predilection does not detract from his point.) "These Circulating Credits have exactly the same effects, in every respect, as an equal quantity of money. As Bishop Berkeley said long ago, a bank is a

---

[270]Henry Dunning Macleod, *The Theory of Credit,* second edition (London: Longman, Green and Co., 1893), vol. I, p. 226.

gold mine. And it is to this faculty, as it were, of multiplying gold that the prodigious advance of commerce and wealth in modern times is entirely due."[271]

Remarking on this misunderstanding, Harvard professor of political economy Charles Dunbar once wrote that "McLeod's [*sic*]remark, that 'every bank is a bank of issue,' may seem a hard saying." And indeed it is. But Dunbar himself displayed admirable awareness of the true state of affairs in his article "Deposits as Currency," from which this quotation was taken.[272] In this article, Dunbar describes how deposits, and the use of checking and other sorts of bank transfer, are actually forms of money creation which, in terms of quantity, by his day (writing in 1887) had outstripped the issue of bank notes. "The fact which it is chiefly desired to emphasize here," he wrote, "is the complete elasticity of this section of our currency. It adapts itself to the demand of the moment without visible effort and either by expansion or contraction, as the case may be; and it does this quite irrespective of legislative purpose or guidance."[273] But there is a caveat to be made. Dunbar emphasizes the importance of bank deposits and their elasticity precisely to provide a counterargument to those who argue for a relaxation of the specie-convertibility requirement. In his view, allowing banks to create deposits while maintaining convertibility serves both ends: to peg the value of the currency to gold, and yet allow the currency to keep pace with expansion. How exactly these two eventualities coexisted, or even could be reconciled, he left undiscussed.

Dunbar's discussion does intimate that banking practice was leaving the security blanket of specie convertibility behind. An economist of the next generation, Herbert J. Davenport, took Dunbar's insight and expanded on it. The reality, says Davenport, is that "the net deposit credits in the national banks in the United States – to say nothing of the other banks – are double the volume of the actual money in the country." "Actual" money would be bank notes and specie, of which a large share "is really employed as reserves to support the credit circulation." And so, "more than 90 per

---

[271]Macleod, *The Theory of Credit* (1897), vol. II, pt. 2, p. 1100.

[272]Charles F. Dunbar, "Deposits as Currency," in *The Quarterly Journal of Economics*, Vol. 1, No. 4 (Jul. 1887), pp. 401-419.

[273]Dunbar, "Deposits as Currency," p. 409.

cent of the larger sorts of transactions are mediated through the use of deposit credit, and probably more than one half of the remaining transactions are similarly effected."[274] The bulk of the circulation therefore comprises created deposits.

This, of course, is contrary to the popular view of deposits; regardless, "it is … a sheer blunder to infer that a bank is rich or strong because of its great total of deposits, or to regard deposits in banking institutions as making part of the aggregate wealth of the community. Instead, the deposits indicate for a bank the extent of its operations, and indicate for a community the extent to which the banks, under the guise of non-interest-bearing obligations, have assumed the debts of business men, on terms of these business men becoming debtors – and interest-paying debtors – to the banks." Davenport's analysis echoes Fisher's. Money created through the "coining" of property means that banks serve an entirely different function than the traditional understanding of deposits would indicate. The bank's strength is not in its cash reserves but in the quality of the collateral put up as security for loans. These are its assets; deposits are its liabilities. "The solvency of the bank is in its portfolio of securities. Its deposits are not its assets, but its liabilities. These liabilities it has mostly created for the use of its borrowers. The further it may safely go in assuming liabilities, the larger its holdings of borrowers' notes may be, and the more interest or discount charges it may collect." What, then, is the function of a bank? To act as a middleman between savers and borrowers? Not at all. "Essentially, therefore, the business of a bank is a form of suretyship – the guaranteeing of its borrowers' solvency – an underwriting of the credit of its customers. The bank transfers its customers' prospective future paying power into present funds. It is for this reason that the contract takes the form of a money loan and the premium the guise of an interest payment."[275]

The noted American economist John Rogers Commons brought this line of reasoning to some degree of fulfillment, by providing a philosophical rationale for it. What Commons saw was that this new system of money

---

[274]H.J. Davenport, *The Economics of Enterprise* (New York: The Macmillan Company, 1913), p. 260.
[275]Davenport, *The Economics of Enterprise*, p. 264.

creation brings the dimension of time into the economic process. Asset-based, debt-generated money creation makes money the function of a collective, market-based understanding of time, or as Commons calls it, futurity. By underlining the role banks play in the entrepreneurial economy as a sort of broker between past, present, and future, Commons takes the analysis one step further.

Commons restricts his analysis of the banking function to business credit – Steuart's mercantile credit – but, in line with Fisher ("so far as the principles here discussed are concerned, they might be any property whatever"),[276] his analysis is valid across the board, for all three forms of debt. "All modern transactions require the participation of bankers," he writes. "Even the 'cash' payments, usually termed the 'circulation of money,' consist in drawing cash from the banks instead of transferring demand debts at the banks. This cash again 'flows' into the banks in payment of debts owed to the banks. The banks themselves, if short on this 'money in circulation,' call upon the Reserve banks for 'money,' thus reducing their balances at the Reserve banks. Or, if long on circulation, they return their 'cash' to the Reserve banks in order to pay debts to the Reserve bank and thus augment their Reserve balances."[277] Therefore, Commons follows Davenport in recognizing that cash actually plays a subordinate role in the total circulation, being used mainly as reserve to meet artificial requirements. This, in turn, is a legacy of the days of specie convertibility, a vestige of the time when "central" banks – actually, monopoly bullion brokers – controlled the money supply through management of the specie base.

How exactly does the banking system create money, then? Commons explains, using the case of business credit: "Out of each possible commercial transaction ... arises the possibility of various types of short-time commercial debts .... All have the one fact in common that the sale of a commodity creates a business debt which the banker buys by selling to the business man his own deposit debt." In other words, the banker buys a bill for payment from the businessman. This bill is owed to the businessman by one of his clients. In exchange for this bill, the banker imputes to the busi-

---

[276]Fisher, *Elementary Principles*, p. 172.
[277]John Rogers Commons, *Institutional Economics: Its Place in Political Economy* (New York: The Macmillan Company, 1934), p. 510.

nessman a deposit which exists only on the bank's books. When the bank
finally receives payment for the bill from the client of the businessman, the
transaction is complete and the loop closed. "The bankers create, in exchange, debts 'past due' and therefore payable on demand, to the extent of
the discounted future value of the business debt, and these deposits are the
checking accounts against which the customer immediately draws his check
for the payment of other debts which he has contracted in his purchases of
materials and labor."[278]

The same thing happens with mortgage loans, but also when the
central bank "monetizes" public debt. A loop is created which is closed
upon final repayment of the original debt. This is the source of the money
supply. "Thus each loan transaction creates its own money. There is not a
fund of money that 'circulates,' but there is a repetition of the creation, sale,
and payment of short-time debts to the amount equivalent to the discounted values of the titles of ownership alienated. Each loan transaction
thus creates its own money, for the banker is an active participant."[279]

Money generated in Steuartian fashion by the modern banking system entails an entirely different theory than a money supply generated from
a central source (either printing or minting). By revealing the decisive implications of the various *forms* of money, Commons made the connection
between monetary practice and theory that has eluded most economists.
"The older controversy over quantity and commodity theories of money
turned on theories of physical causation in which it was thought that the
event first in order of time was the cause of the event subsequent, and the
statistical proof or disproof turned on showing whether a change in the
quantity of money preceded or followed, a change in prices." Although
Commons does not mention this, such a theory of money followed from a
central-source money supply. At any rate, it follows from a physically existing, externalized money supply. For a dispersed, representative, asset-based
money supply, another theory is requisite: "a transactional or forecast theory of money and prices is a theory of the transfer, not of goods, but of
proprietary control of expected goods, since the goods come along later.

---

[278]Commons, *Institutional Economics*, pp. 510-511.
[279]Commons, *Institutional Economics*, p. 511.

The value agreed upon is the price of acquiring rights of ownership, and this price is always a forecast of the immediate or remote future. This kind of causation lies in the future, not in the past or present." Money generated through the agency of banks is money issued in terms of an appraisal of future opportunity, not past accumulation – a fundamental difference. "Hence the appropriate doctrine of cause and effect is found in billions of transactions, where the banker who creates the money participates as a guide to the transaction. While the engineer is the specialist in efficiency, and the business man is the specialist in scarcity, the banker is the specialist in futurity."[280]

Therefore money is an instrument of time and future expectations, arising, circulating, and expiring in a constantly repeating cycle, all in service of a dynamic economy. It is an artificial creation, an institution, not a pre-existing thing. "The foregoing indicates that money, in its modern meaning, is the social institution of the creation, negotiability, and release of debts arising out of transactions.... But if, as a social institution, each loan trans-action creates its own money and the whole volume is created and extin-guished every 30 days, then *the definition of money should be converted from the static idea of a quantity to the dynamic idea of a process.* The process is the billions of bargaining transactions, with the bankers as participants."[281] Of course, in the case of longer-term loans, the volume recycles over a longer period, but the idea is the same. The focus is no longer on quantities, on "sub-stance," as the philosophers use to say, but on dynamic processes, on ever-shifting fluxes.

The process of engaging and extinguishing credit and debt, then, underlies the money supply, which itself is nothing more than the snapshot at any particular time of ephemeral quanta. Commons, quite aware of this, argued for the need of a different language to describe it, and thus for a change of key in economic theory:

> We take it that a process is more accurately described when verbs are substituted for nouns. Nouns are likely to be misleading

---

[280]Commons, *Institutional Economics*, pp. 511-512.
[281]Commons, *Institutional Economics*, p. 512. Italics added.

because they give the impression of static quantities, but verbal nouns are fitted to the bargaining transactions which are none other than the process of pricing, valuing, and debiting, which create, transfer, extinguish, and recreate both economic quantities and the money which measures them as values. The price, the value, the debt, are each jointly determined, if not literally created, at the point of time when the agreement transfers the ownership of the economic quantity thus agreed upon, and all the variabilities, taken together in the sequence of time, are a process of pricing, valuing, and debiting by means of transactions.[282]

This kind of monetary system puts the economic order on an entirely new plane: the regime of scarcity is exchanged for the regime of abundance. It is interesting that Commons, whose economics can be characterized as the economics of abundance as opposed to scarcity (although he applied the terms in another context), was also a specialist in labor economics, and edited the first history of the labor movement in America. Perhaps it was his close involvement with the labor movement that led him to realize the importance of the shift in money-supply orientation. Perhaps he had already answered for himself that burning question among progressives, first asked by Werner Sombart in 1906: why is there no socialism in the United States?[283]

It is the real-life realization of Russell Conwell's popular parable from the 19th century, "Acres of Diamonds." In the parable, the protagonist sells his property in order to seek wealth, whether diamonds, gold, or oil, in far-away places; but the one who buys the property discovers precisely the thing the original owner had sought – on the original property. And so, "the idea is that in this country of ours every man has the opportunity to make more of himself than he [already] does in his own environment, with his own skill, with his own energy, and with his own friends."[284] This is the

---

[282]Commons, *Institutional Economics,* pp. 512-513.

[283]Werner Sombart, *Why Is There No Socialism in the United States?* translated by Patricia M. Hocking and C.T. Husbands; edited and with an introductory essay by C.T. Husbands and with a foreword by Michael Harrington (London: Macmillan, 1976 [1906]).

[284]Russell H. Conwell, *Acres of Diamonds* (New York and London: Harper &

archetypal parable for 19th-century America, given its promise of prosperity not through feverish attempts to find refuge from an unyielding, unforgiving environment, but simply through recognizing, and acting on, hitherto unrecognized opportunities, staring one, as it were, in the face.

Brothers Publishers, 1915), p. 2.

" Exactly so !   I am a humbug."

Figure 25: The Wizard of Oz unmasked. From L. Frank Baum, *The Wonderful Wizard of Oz*, pictures by W.W. Denslow (Chicago & New York: Geo. M. Hill Co., 1900).

19. THE RUBY SLIPPERS

John Rogers Commons is one of the few economists to have recognized the difference between abundance and scarcity orientations. His path-breaking analysis has gone entirely unrecognized, at least in terms of theory. Practice, of course, followed his lead, which is another way of saying that he paid sufficient attention to practice to follow *its* lead.

Economic policy today is informed by obsolete economic theory geared in two directions, answering to left-wing and right-wing political agendas. These vie with the actual needs of the world's economies – based as they are in organic, spontaneous development that has charged ahead without regard to the theories of politicians, policymakers, or academics.

The Left is engaged in a disconcerting scramble to establish and preserve vested interests, such as labor union entitlements. It is a situation reminiscent of the mercantilist age of privilege, in which vested interests were peddled by the crown and used by it to solidify its own power (the "royal mechanism" – see p. 68). That system was shunted aside by the automatic mechanism, but it was reborn when labor tired of bearing the brunt of deflationary swings, became organized, and retooled the "royal mechanism," in order to fight mechanism with mechanism.[285] It is a legacy of the times of currency scarcity. It may yet win elections, but it cannot solve problems. It is a strategy fit only to rearrange deck chairs on a sinking ship.

The Right denigrates "Keynesianism," by which they mean Monetarist Keynesianism (discussed above) with its pump-priming intended to stimulate economic growth. Central banking as embodied in the Federal Reserve is viewed as a debt-laundering operation enabling the government to run up an ever more onerous debt burden. Many favor a return to the gold standard to put government back within proper spending boundaries. There is also a castigation of the Left's pursuit of vested interests precisely because they restrict freedom of trade, both domestically and internation-

---

[285]For a description of the deleterious effects of the modern-day "royal mechanism," see Alvarado, *Common Law & Natural Rights,* ch. 2, "The Broken Machinery."

ally. Therefore, many on the right are simply knee-jerk representatives of the free-market nostrums peddled in the 19th century by the very banking interests conservatives now profess to abhor.

The disconnect between theory and reality has come home to roost in the ongoing credit crisis. As outlined in the introduction, many view this crisis as being the result of the greed of bankers and financiers. What actually happened was that bankers and financiers were struggling to break even within the context of a near-zero interest rate lending situation. Investors were pulling money out of savings and into active investment, resulting in a massive amount of funds seeking profitable employment. This in turn put pressure on portfolio managers to generate returns, leading to the progressive development of increasingly inventive investment products, including the packaging of subprime loans in so-called Collateralized Debt Obligations (CDOs).[286] The low-interest-rate environment also fostered the notion of zero risk, leading to ever-greater risk-taking; here again, it was not greed but the desire to turn a profit within a saturated investment environment that was behind this willingness to shoulder ever-greater risk burdens.

This low-interest-rate environment was itself the unique result of a return to interest-rate pegging. The original regime of loosely-pegged exchange rates collapsed in 1971, when President Nixon severed the link between the dollar and gold. There followed a chaotic period of inflation and depreciation which seemed to beg for a return to exchange-rate stability. The United States experienced a period of years of high inflation, which was only turned around by the drastic action of Fed chairman Paul Volcker during the Reagan presidency.[287] Developing countries like Brazil and Ar-

---

[286]"These instruments do not deserve the term 'collateral' in their names. Yet, insufficiently collateralised debt obligations (ICDOs) would not have been an easy sell." Gunnar Heinsohn and Otto Steiger, "Collateral and Own Capital: The Missing Links in the Theory of the Rate of Interest and of Money," in Steiger, ed., *Property Economics: Property Rights, Creditor's Money and the Foundations of the Economy* (Marburg, Germany: Metropolis Verlag, 2008), p. 217.

[287]A good description of this chain of events is contained in William Greider, *Secrets of the Temple: How the Federal Reserve Runs the Country* (New York: Simon & Schuster, 1989). Of course, the Federal Reserve does not run the country. Its open-market operations determine the level of short-term interest rates; for the rest, its effect is more apparent than real – often enough, mere smoke and mirrors.

gentina went through years of astronomical inflation. Debt incurred by developing countries during periods of relatively stable exchange rates, when their currencies held parity against first-world currencies, had to be repaid in those first-world currencies, even as the country's own currency rapidly depreciated – an impossible task, which in its own way recalled the worst effects of the gold-based system.

In the 1990s, most countries were able to consolidate their fiscal and monetary positions, thus leaving behind the period of massive inflation and depreciation. But beyond this, there came a renewed desire to peg exchange rates, as a means to achieve "stability." In Europe, this led to the coalescing of exchange rates across a broad swath of countries, anchored on the deutschmark. Together with China's pegging of the exchange rate of the yuan to the dollar at an artificially low level, this led to the low-interest-rate environment that fostered the investment bubble.

At this time, the euro and the yuan continue to foster an artificial exchange-rate climate that has generated global imbalances and sluggish growth. The disengagement (untangling) of exchange rates will be a key element to any sustained recovery from the present economic malaise.

The European Union's monetary system constitutes a return to fixed exchange rates very similar to the time of the gold standard, with something of an automatic mechanism whereby flows of currency and capital are left relatively unrestricted. Capital investments and loans are thus secure from currency risk as well as, in the case of loans, from the risk of default, thanks to the European Central Bank and European Monetary System (EMS). This has spurred lending and other forms of investment to all parts of the European Union on a massive scale.

The debt burden in the European Union is becoming unbearable because the founders of the fixed-exchange rate system forgot what it was that made the gold-standard system founder: fixed exchange rates do not allow differing rates of economic productivity to find expression in exchange rates, and thus strangle economic growth. In an amalgamation of economic areas that do not share the same level of economic "competitive advantage" – say, Germany on the one hand and Spain on the other – the divergence in productivity will not be offset by shifts in exchange rates, the way in which such would take place in floating exchange-rate regime. Instead, the fixed-exchange rate system tends toward a center-periphery arrangement – paradigmatic "colonialism" – whereby the more-productive area uses the less-productive area as a market for its goods, while funding the purchases of those goods through lending, ostensibly guaranteed by the EMS, but in the end unsustainable.[288]

Such a situation is moving towards its inexorable climax at the moment of writing (Autumn 2012), with the great difference that each of the member nations – which as of now are still semi-sovereign nations – has its own welfare-state apparatus shielding its citizenry from the ravages of the fixed-exchange rate regime. But this very regime stands in the way of the kind of adjustment a fixed-exchange rate regime requires, namely, wage declines within a deflationary environment. Johan van Overtveldt makes this clear regarding the Greek situation: "The traditional way out of such a vicious cycle is currency devaluation, which boosts external demand and stimulates internal production. Of course, devaluation is not an option in a monetary union. With international competitiveness way out of line, a devaluation-like effect can be achieved through a massive internal deflation with nominal wage cuts. Whether Greece could survive such a hellish combination of deficit cutting and internal deflation was very much in doubt."[289] Just such a regime is precisely what called the entire labor movement into being in the first place. Europe is being asked either to sacrifice labor (and production in general) to the creditor class, or to sacrifice the creditor class by returning to floating exchange rates.

Furthermore, the lack of economic growth – itself the result of being hitched to another economy's (read: Germany's) wagon – has led to mounting debt burdens with no relief in sight. The way out of the impasse is to generate economic growth, and the only way to generate economic growth is to return to floating exchange rates, allowing the currency, and thus the importing/exporting economy, to find equilibrium vis-a-vis trading partners. But this would leave creditors high and dry, for having lent in euros,

---

[288]This dynamic has been described in detail by Jason Manolopoulos, *Greece's 'Odious' Debt: The Looting of the Hellenic Republic by the Euro, the Political Elite and the Investment Community* (London and New York: Anthem Press, 2011).

[289]Johan van Overtveldt, *The End of the Euro: The Uneasy Future of the European Union* (Chicago: B2 Books, 2011), p. 96; see also p. 151.

they expect to be paid back in euros. That would include the major banks of Europe. The solution to this crisis has yet to present itself.

In contrast to the "New Normal" of low growth and burgeoning debt in the First World countries, there has been a major turnaround under way among emerging countries, dating from the late 1990s. These countries have put their fiscal and economic houses in order, and are now sporting economic fundamentals that put First-World countries in Europe and North America to shame. Having written extensively about this in my book *Investing in the New Normal*, it remains only to point out how the realities there expounded are the end-result of the developments sketched in this book.

Hernando de Soto, the Peruvian champion of free-market economics among developing countries, has for years pointed out the need for what can only be seen as a Steuartian solution to the economic problems of those developing countries. Top-down, government-provided solutions have only exacerbated the problem, he writes, because they grew government rather than the grass roots. In fact, government regulatory restrictions, implemented in a corrupt manner, have been the main factor hindering economic growth – this was De Soto's passionate plea. It is not that the common people are useless, lazy, and incompetent; it is that they are not given a chance to provide a better life for themselves. The absence of proper institutions is behind the absence of opportunity.

The requisite institutions are mainly legal, revolving around property and contract – in other words, private law. If governments would focus on providing basic justice to all its citizens in these crucial areas, and clean up their acts with regard to corruption, bribery, and the like, these countries could provide for themselves and begin the climb to self-sustaining economic growth. In De Soto's view, a crucial aspect of this development would be property registration – what he calls formalization of property rights – which would put property on settled foundations and enable property-owners, be they merely holders of small plots of land with shacks for dwellings, to obtain credit on security of their property.

This is indeed what is going on, in increasing degree, in developing countries today. Along with governments that are living within their means, and growing corporate sectors providing quality mercantile credit and debt, the money supplies in these countries are coming into sync with the economic needs, accurately reflecting the asset base against which money is issued. This results in both economic growth and low, stable inflation rates, the necessary prerequisites of healthy economies.

De Soto described this as "the Mystery of Capital:" how it was that Western countries achieved economic growth while the rest of the world remained mired in poverty.[290] But he missed the crucial connecting link, the one that Steuart already put forward: the role of banks as, in Commons' words, "experts in futurity," the brokers between future expectations, present constraints, and past performance. It is their role of creating deposits in response to demand and in terms of good securities – embedded, of course, within the framework of property and contract, without which none of this could arise – which is the *sine qua non* to a functioning grass-roots economy.[291]

The scholars who have done the most to restore this connecting link to economic theory in our day are the German trio of Heinsohn, Steiger, and Stadermann. They all emphasize the origin of money in credit contracts, although they overemphasize the role of central banks in this process. Nevertheless, they provide a wealth of fundamental insights helpful to piercing the veil of ignorance that enshrouds contemporary economics regarding money.

It reminds one strongly of the children's story *The Wonderful Wizard of Oz*, originally written by L. Frank Baum and later made into one of the most famous movies of all time. The original story may well have been written as an allegory of the conflict over silver and gold standards that culminated in the 1890s,[292] but regardless, the symbolism is illuminating.

---

[290]Hernando de Soto, *The Mystery of Capital: Why Capitalism Triumphs in the West and Fails Everywhere Else* (New York: Basic Books, 2000).

[291]De Soto's emphasis on property registration leads him to misread entirely the history of 19th century US economic development, as if it were analogous to the "extralegal" situation in Third-World countries today. A common-law system is not "extralegal," and the crucial role played by banks in grass-roots economic development in America is something of which De Soto does not even appear to be aware. See e.g. Howard Bodenhorn, *State Banking in Early America: A New Economic History* (Oxford: Oxford University Press, 2003).

[292]Favoring the allegory thesis: Hugh Rockoff, "The 'Wizard of Oz' as Monetary Allegory," in *Journal of Political Economy*, Vol. 98, No. 4 (Aug., 1990), pp.

Each of the characters resorts to the Wizard of Oz (who turns out to be a "humbug" – Ben Bernanke, anyone?) to grant them a wish, which, had they only known better, they would know they already had. The Scarecrow desires a brain above all things, but – and the book is much clearer on this than the movie – he demonstrates good sense and good thinking throughout the journey. The same holds true for the Tin Woodman (who desires a heart), and the Cowardly Lion (who desires courage). Even Dorothy from the beginning possesses the capacity to return to Kansas, in the form of her ruby slippers.[293] But because of their ignorance, they are led to follow the "Yellow Brick Road" – the gold standard, it would seem – to gain an imaginary fulfillment that in the end turns out to be, well, humbug.

And so it has been in the history of money and economic performance. The precious metals have been viewed as indispensable to attaining prosperity, even to embodying that prosperity. And indeed, their role as universally recognized store of value has enabled them to fulfill a bridge-building, culture- and sovereignty-spanning function linking the disparate fragments of humanity into a more or less coherent partnership in a common enterprise. Their successes in this led mankind to believe them to be indispensable, making them (and their controllers) the master of man. Mankind was blinded to the fact that this was only a role, one that might be superseded through institutions of law that are the creation, and thus the servant, of man. In his famous speech to the Democratic National Convention in 1896, William Jennings Bryan thundered it out: "Having behind us the producing masses of this nation and the world, supported by the commercial interests, the laboring interests, and the toilers everywhere, we will answer their demand for a gold standard by saying to them: 'You shall not press down upon the brow of labor this crown of thorns; you shall not crucify mankind upon a cross of gold.'" The sentiment was thoroughly justified. Currency is a means, an instrument, a tool, no more and no less. It does not do to put the tool over the one who wields it.

739-760; opposing it: Bradley A. Hansen, "The Fable of the Allegory: The Wizard of Oz in Economics," in *The Journal of Economic Education*, Vol. 33, No. 3 (Summer, 2002), pp. 254-264.

[293]In the book, Dorothy's slippers are silver, which gives added cachet to the money-allegory hypothesis.

Through the institutions of property and contract, credit and debt, the asset base *in* man (human capital) and *through* man (tangible and intangible property) becomes capitalized, generating a money supply which, when properly maintained, is the faithful representation of that asset base, no more and no less. The nations of the world have no need of a Wizard of Oz to grant them prosperity. It is in their hands to do so, if they would only recognize it. And increasingly, it seems they have. For the rest, because of faulty theory, some nations seem to have forgotten the lesson before they ever really had the chance to appreciate it.

20. BIBLIOGRAPHIC ESSAY

As indicated in the introduction, the work of many scholars has been put to use in the making of this book. The following will be an attempt to indicate the most important sources consulted in its writing. Because the subject matter is so varied and involves so many areas of study, these sources are necessarily wide-ranging. There is (as yet) no study of money such as is conducted, in however rudimentary a fashion, in this book. There are areas of study focusing on various aspects of money (such as numismatics) but none *effectively* on money as such, as a subject of study in its own right. The various books that have been written purporting to provide such have all proven to be *ineffective,* because they invariably work in terms of a deficient theoretical basis, causing them to overlook essential matters and to truncate and distort what ought to be presented with clarity and openness.

Some examples of this sort of book would be G.F. Knapp, *The State Theory of Money;* Karl Knies, *Money and Credit;* Karl Helfferich, *Money;* Ludwig von Mises, *The Theory of Money and Credit.* This list could be greatly extended. Nevertheless, it is not my intention to provide a comprehensive overview of the literature but rather to give an indication of this radical shortfall. The books listed above all fall short because none of them have a comprehensive understanding of what money is. In this essay, my purpose is merely to indicate the texts I found to be important in developing the argument of this book.

Oddly enough, the various works covering the history of money did not prove to be of any great value in this regard. One exception was Pierre Vilar, *A History of Gold and Money 1450-1920,* trans. Judith White (London: NLB, 1976). Another helpful work, albeit in German: Michael North, *Das Geld und seine Geschichte: Vom Mittelalter bis zur Gegenwart* (Munich: Verlag C.H. Beck, 1994). Both of these books commence with the late-medieval period. For history prior to that, one must refer either to the specialist literature or to the books listed below regarding coinage.

The work that first opened my eyes to a Steuartian view of money was provided by the German trio of Gunnar Heinsohn, Otto Steiger, and Hans-Joachim Stadermann. The seminal text here is provided by Heinsohn and Steiger: *Property, Interest, and Money: Unsolved Riddles of Economic Science* [Eigentum, Zins, und Geld: Ungelöste Rätsel der Wirtschaftwissenschaft] (Marburg: Metropolis Verlag, 2011 [7th edition]). The first edition was published in 1996. It was apparently to be published in translation by Routledge in 2006, but nothing, it seems, has come of this. What the book contains, in essence, is a Steuartian understanding of money as symbolical, created through credit contracts and representative of the collateral put up to secure it. It includes extended and thorough critiques of all the major streams of economic science, but has one major shortcoming: it views all forms of money through the lens of symbolical money, and thus discounts the existence either of commodity-based money or state-issued fiduciary money. Nevertheless, there is much to learn from it, along with the other publications this German triumvirate have put forward. English translations of various articles are available in John Smithin, *What is Money?* (London: Routledge, 2000); Jürgen Georg Backhaus, *Handbook of the History of Economic Thought: Insights on the Founders of Modern Economics* (New York: Springer, 2011); Otto Steiger (ed.), *Property Economics: Property Rights, Creditor's Money and the Foundations of the Economy* (Marburg: Metropolis Verlag, 2008).

    Steuart's key role is specifically highlighted in Hans-Joachim Stadermann and Otto Steiger, "James Steuart and the Theory of the Monetary Economy," in Jürgen Georg Backhaus (ed.), *Handbook of the History of Economic Thought: Insights on the Founders of Modern Economics* (New York: Springer, 2011), pp. 667-688; Stadermann and Steiger, *Allgemeine Theorie der Wirtschaft: Erster Band, Schulökonomik* [General Theory of Economics: Volume 1, Scholastic Economics] (Tübingen: Mohr Siebeck, 2001).

    Of course, the main book to consult as far as Steuartian money and banking is concerned is the one written by Sir James Steuart himself. His major work is *An Inquiry Into the Principles of Political Oeconomy: Being an Essay on the Science of Domestic Policy in Free Nations. In Which are Particularly Considered Population, Agriculture, Trade, Industry, Money, Coin, Interest, Circulation, Banks, Exchange, Public Credit, and Taxes* (London: Printed for A. Millar and T. Cadell, 1767), in two volumes. There are no modern versions of the book available. There is a modernized digital text available online, although it is a) strewn with the typical errors that crop up in optical-character recognition,

b) drops sections of text (even within specific paragraphs), and c) leaves out entire chapters.

David Graeber's *Debt: The First 5,000 Years* (New York: Melville House Books, 2011) is excellent for its presentation of the correlation of money and debt, and its debunking of the myth of the barter origin of money. As Graeber brilliantly puts it, "Barter … appears to be largely a kind of accidental byproduct of the use of coinage or paper money: historically, it has mainly been what people who are used to cash transactions do when for one reason or another they have no access to currency" (p. 40). An anthropologist, Graeber shows that debt is primordial, it is woven into the warp and woof of society, and it is indeed inescapable.

One of the benefits of Graeber's book is its succinct presentation of ancient Mesopotamian banking practice (see p. 15ff. above). Regarding ancient Sumerian and Babylonian banking, the literature is specialized and abstruse. Beyond the works cited in the text above, the material cited in Graeber may be consulted. Further, Morris Silver, *Economic Structures of Antiquity* (Westport CT: Greenwood Press, 1995) contains a helpful discussion on credit and banking as well as debt slavery.

David Astle's *The Babylonian Woe: A Study of the Origin of Certain Banking Practices, and of their effect on the events of Ancient History, written in the light of the Present Day* (n.p., 1975), is brilliant in its idiosyncratic, speculative interpretation of ancient banking practice. Astle understood the working of fractional-reserve banking very well and put forward a plausible scenario for its functioning in the ancient world. However, his work is vitiated by a penchant for over-speculation, as well as his complete misreading of the role of coinage.

Regarding coinage, the best books by way of introduction are Christopher Howgego, *Ancient History From Coins* (London: Routledge, 1995); Peter Spufford, *Money and Its Use in Medieval Europe* (Cambridge: Cambridge University Press, 1988). Spufford's book is not only good on medieval coinage, it helps to frame the subject of coinage in its entirety. Other authors of great help in this area are John Day and John Munro. Dr. Munro's work has the great benefit of being available online in copious amounts.[294] Regarding

---

[294]e.g., http://www.economics.utoronto.ca/munro5/WorkingPapers.htm.

the fiduciary character of ancient Greek coinage, see Richard Seaford, *Money and the Early Greek Mind: Homer, Philosophy, Tragedy* (Cambridge: Cambridge University Press, 2004). I would also be remiss not to mention the following authors, whose work likewise was very helpful, especially their contributions to the Cambridge Histories: Philip Grierson, Mark Blackburn, and Mireille Corbier.

"Dark Age" early medieval economics is undergoing a sea change thanks to the contribution of archaeology, especially in the area of numismatics (this also holds true for late-imperial Rome). The discussion on pages 58 and following is based on the work of Richard Hodges as contained in *Dark Age Economics: The Origins of Towns and Trade A.D. 600-1000*, second edition (Bristol Classical Press, 2011); *Mohammed, Charlemagne, and the Origins of Europe: The Pirenne Thesis in the Light of Archaeology* (Ithaca: Cornell University Press, 1983); and *Towns and Trade in the Age of Charlemagne* (London: Duckworth, 2000), as well as the debate Hodges' work has inspired. The space allocated to this subject in the text is no good indicator of its importance.

Alexander Del Mar's work is subject to the same appraisal as Astle's: brilliant insight combined with over-speculation and dodgy details. But it is to Del Mar, and in particular *Money and Civilization* (London: George Bell and Sons, 1886), that we owe the crucial insight into the shift in monetary policy in early modern England away from coinage and toward commodity money, and what that meant for the Money Power. Del Mar's unerring instinct put him on to the crucial difference between commodity money and coinage; nevertheless, he did not recognize the third member of the monetary triumvirate, Steuartian bank money.

On early American banking, the key texts are Robert E. Wright, *Origins of Commercial Banking in America, 1750-1800* (Lanham, MD: Rowman & Littlefield Publishers, Inc., 2001); Howard Bodenhorn, *State Banking in Early America: A New Economic History* (Oxford: Oxford University Press, 2003); and, above all, Bray Hammond, *Banks and Politics in America: From the Revolution to the Civil War* (Princeton: Princeton University Press, 1957). Hammond's book is an excellent introduction to the entire subject of modern banking, albeit – and this is endemic – it overemphasizes and miscasts the role of central banks. Wright's comments in the introduction to his book, dismissing the importance of Hammond's book, appear to have been written in a spirit of aversion to Hammond's monetary philosophy rather than an objective appraisal of the book's value. Hammond was something of a Keynesian, while Wright is something of an Austrian-school classical economist. Bodenhorn's book is excellent in its discussion of the forms of collateral used in early American "free" banking, demonstrating just how Steuartian – my characterization, not his – banking practice was.

For the gold standard and modern civilization, Carroll Quigley's *Tragedy and Hope: A History of the World in Our Time* (New York: Macmillan, 1966) is required reading. The firestorm this book provoked, mainly because of its use by conspiracy theorists to establish the existence of an omnipotent Money Power that to this day controls world affairs, led to its being placed on waivers, as it were, by respectable scholars, which is entirely absurd, and only contributes to confirm such notions of conspiracy. One tidbit I have always found interesting is that, in the index, the reference to "Banking and bankers" is found, not in its alphabetically-ordered place, but rather, in some form of rare misprint, between "Brown, W. A." and "Brown Brothers & Harriman." Whether this was intentional or not, we may never know.

Other serious works, full of useful information, critical of the gold standard and written during and just after its heyday, include Brooks Adams, *The Law of Civilization and Decay: An Essay on History*, 2nd ed. (New York: The Macmillan Company, 1897); Christopher Hollis, *The Two Nations: A Financial Study of English History* (London: George Routledge & Sons, 1935); Robert McNair Wilson, *Monarchy or Money Power*, 2nd edition (London: Eyre & Spottiswoode, 1934). Adams in particular is full of brilliant insights, although combined, one might almost say inevitably, with far-fetched hypotheses, such as the Industrial Revolution in England being sparked by the plunder of Bengal. Interestingly, both Hollis and McNair Wilson wrote from a Roman Catholic perspective, comparing medieval civilization favorably with modern industrialism; in their view, democracy is inevitably plutocracy, while only monarchy can provide sound currency.

Regarding the economics of scarcity versus the economics of abundance, it should be made clear that the kind of economics of abundance I have in mind is the kind put forward in such books as George Gilder, *Wealth and Poverty: A New Edition for the Twenty-First Century* (Washington, DC: Regnery Publishing, Inc., 2012 [original edition 1981]). It is *not* that put forward in Brendan Sheehan, *The Economics of Abundance: Affluent Consump-tion and the Global Economy* (Cheltenham, UK, et al: Edward Elgar, 2010), which takes up the line of thought expounded by John Kenneth Galbraith in *The Affluent Society* (Boston: Houghton Mifflin, 1958), and is essentially the economics of excess, not abundance. There is a difference.

For the rest, the works cited in the text are all worthy of consulta-tion.

21. INDEX

NOTE: Subjects that appear throughout the text are not listed here. These include gold, silver, money, law, and property.